BRE 17147   941.082

D0238359

history at source

BRITAIN *1900–1945*

Ron Stapley

Hodder & Stoughton

LONDON SYDNEY AUCKLAND

The cover illustration is an election poster used by the Labour Party in 1910 and 1929.

British Library Cataloguing in Publication Data
Stapley, R F.
  Britain, 1900–45. – (History at Source Series)
  I. Title   II. Series
  941.082

ISBN 0–340–56546–2

First published 1992

© 1992 Ron Stapley

All rights reserved. No part of this publication may be reproduced or
transmitted in any form or by any means, electronic or mechanical,
including photocopy, recording, or any information storage and
retrieval system, without permission in writing from the publisher
or under licence from the Copyright Licensing Agency Limited.
Further details of such licences (for reprographic reproduction)
may be obtained from the Copyright Licensing Agency Limited, of
90 Tottenham Court Road, London W1P 9HE.

Typeset by Litho Link Ltd, Welshpool, Powys, Wales.
Printed in Great Britain for the educational publishing
division of Hodder & Stoughton Ltd, Mill Road, Dunton Green,
Sevenoaks, Kent by Page Bros (Norwich) Ltd.

CONTENTS

PREFACE

British twentieth-century history has always been a popular topic among those studying at A Level or Higher Grade, and beyond, and it is likely to attract candidates for AS Level. The period after 1945 may be both politically and historically controversial, but the period before 1945 has attracted much historical literature, and it is rich in argument, making its study interesting but demanding. Changes in the requirements of examination boards add to the demands on students and teachers, particularly in the field of source-based questions, coursework and personal assignments.

This book is intended for students and, it is to be hoped, teachers who are interested in British twentieth-century domestic history before 1945, and who would welcome a practical complement to existing textbooks and monographs. A number of central issues and topics are introduced through collections of primary and secondary sources, together with questions of the type likely to be encountered in examinations, or other exercises involving the use of sources. Practical advice is offered on the way to approach such questions, and a specimen answer is included. Guidance is also offered on the approach to essay questions, and some attempt is made to classify them according to type. Sample essay titles are given along with suggestions for relevant approaches, and again, a specimen answer is included. Finally, a brief analytical bibliography is intended to give guidance to students and teachers alike.

It is hoped that this collection will prove useful for students working as part of an organised course, or on their own.

APPROACHING SOURCE-BASED

QUESTIONS

Source-based questions have become an important part of History examinations at all levels in recent years. Students who have studied History at GCSE and Standard Grade will be used to handling various types of sources. The skills they have learned in dealing with evidence will continue to be applicable at a more advanced level, but there will also be more sophisticated skills to master and the sources themselves will certainly be more demanding.

During your studies you will encounter both primary and secondary historical evidence. The distinction between the two is sometimes artificially exaggerated: all sources have their value and limitations and it is possible to worry unnecessarily about a 'hierarchy of sources'. The important thing is for the student to feel confident in handling all sources. The majority of sources in this book are primary sources, since they are the raw material from which historians work; and they are mostly of a documentary nature, because that is the type most commonly found in examinations. However, there are also statistics and examples of visual evidence. The comments below will usually apply to *all* types of evidence.

When a student is faced with a piece of historical evidence, there are certain questions that he or she should always ask of that source; but in an examination that student will be asked specific questions set by an examiner, and, in the light of pressures, not least of which is time, it is important to approach these questions in an organised and coherent fashion. The following advice should be borne in mind when answering source-based questions. Some of the advice may appear obvious in the cold light of day, but, as examiners will testify, the obvious is often ignored in the heat of the examination room!

1   Read the sources carefully before attempting to answer the questions, whether there is one source or a collection of them. This will give you an overview of the sources which will usually be connected and related to a particular theme. You will study the individual sources in detail when you answer specific questions.

2   Always look carefully at the attribution of the sources: the author and date of publication; the recipient, if any; the context in which the source was produced. All these will often give you an insight in addition to that provided by the content of the source itself.

3   Mark allocations are usually given at the end of each question or sub-question. Ignore the marks at your peril! The number of marks will

almost certainly give you some indication of the length of the answer expected. Length of answer is not an indicator of quality, and there is no such thing as a standard answer, but it is commonplace for candidates in examinations to write paragraph-length answers to questions offering one or two marks. A question carrying such a low mark can usually be adequately answered in two or three sentences. You do not have time to waste your purple prose in examinations! Similarly, a mark allocation of nine or ten marks indicates the expectation of a reasonably substantial answer.

4   Read *all* the parts of a question through before attempting it. In your enthusiasm you may stray outside the limits of the first sub-question unless you have seen from subsequent sub-questions that material you thought relevant to sub-question (a) is, in fact, far more appropriate to sub-question (b) or (c). Study the wording of the questions very carefully. Some questions will ask you to use *only* your own knowledge in the answer; some will ask you to use *both* your own knowledge *and* the source(s); some will insist that you confine your answer to knowledge gleaned from the source(s) *alone*. If you ignore the instructions, you will certainly deprive yourself of marks.

5   If there are several sources to be consulted, ensure that you make use of the ones to which you are directed – candidates have been known to ignore some or choose the wrong ones!

6   Certain types of question require a particular type of response:

(a) Comparison of and/or contrasting sources: ensure that you do consider all the sources required by the question.
(b) Testing the usefulness and limitations of sources: if you are asked to do both, ensure that you do consider both aspects. You may be required to evaluate a source in relation to other information provided, or in the context of your own background knowledge of the subject.
(c) Testing reliability: this is not the same as considering the usefulness of a source, although students sometimes confuse the two concepts.
(d) Phrases such as 'Comment upon', 'Analyse' or 'Assess': ensure that you do what is asked. Do not be afraid of quoting extracts from a source in your answer, but avoid over-quotation or too much paraphrasing, since questions will usually, although not always, be testing more than comprehension. Your direct use of the sources should therefore be illustrating or amplifying a particular point, e.g. direct quotation of words and phrases to illustrate bias. Always *use* the sources and do not just regurgitate what is in front of you.
(e) Synthesis: this is a high level skill which requires you to blend several pieces of evidence and draw general conclusions.

7   If at all possible, avoid spending too much time on the sources questions in examinations. Frequently candidates answer the sources questions thoroughly but do not allow themselves enough time to do justice to the rest of the examination paper, and essay answers sometimes suffer in consequence. Nevertheless, it is still best to tackle the source questions first, rather than last, provided that you allocate the time for each question sensibly.

8   If possible, read published examiners' reports which will give you further indication as to the most useful approaches to particular questions, and the pitfalls to avoid.

A note on this Collection of Sources

It is the intention of this collection to give ideas to teachers and realistic examples of sources and questions to students, either for use in schools and colleges or for self-study. However, they are intended to be flexible. If it is found helpful, adapt the questions or mark allocations, or devise new questions; or use the sources as part of coursework or personal studies. You might even find it an interesting exercise to put together your own sources and appropriate questions.

1 CONSERVATISM ON THE
DEFENSIVE 1900–1905

Economic historians date Britain's industrial and commercial decline from as far back as the 1870s. But to the country at large and to the politicians, Britain appeared to be at the peak of her greatness as the twentieth century opened. The South African War, which in December 1899 had given cause for alarm, seemed a year later to be drawing to a successful close; the British Empire encompassed a quarter of the globe; British goods dominated world markets; and newspaper editorials on 1 January 1901 marvelled at Britain's industrial and social progress during the last half century. There was much smug self-satisfaction about political progress, too, even though less than two thirds of males had the franchise. Many felt optimistic about the future.

A few dissenting voices were raised. The Fabians and the Independent Labour Party on the left, and Rowntree at York, drew attention to gross social inequalities and grinding poverty. But these were on the fringes of the political stage. The Second Boer War had united the vast majority of the nation in an upsurge of patriotism and imperialism, and the Conservative Party had taken advantage of the prevailing mood to win for itself a large majority in the 'Khaki Election' in 1900. The Liberal Party owed much of its disarray to its commitment to Home Rule for Ireland, and the opposition of some of its radicals like Lloyd George to the Boer War.

Nevertheless, the prolonged war in South Africa did lead to some questioning of imperialism, and the Conservative government of Lord Salisbury came under criticism for dragging its feet on necessary social reform. Conservative difficulties were similar to those of any party which had been in power for a long time, and it would hardly have expected to repeat the success of 1900 when the next general election became due. Yet the party's main wounds were self-inflicted. Joseph Chamberlain was neither a visionary nor a prophet. He did not propose 'tariff reform' to protect Britain from economic decline. His main concern was to consolidate and bind the Empire in economic unity, and to use an Imperial Tariff against countries like Germany which had discriminated against Canadian goods. Balfour, prime minister on Salisbury's retirement in 1902, neither supported Chamberlain nor disowned him. But he allowed Chamberlain to resign in September 1903 and at the same time removed die-hard free traders from his Cabinet. The Conservatives were now divided, and Balfour compounded his questionable tactics on tariff reform by resigning with his Cabinet in December 1905. He may have hoped that this would shift the spotlight from Conservative divisions to Liberal ones, but the Liberals immediately called a general election, and won a great landslide victory.

There may well have been unique and special factors working in the Liberals' favour in 1906, but Chamberlain's persistence in splitting the party, and Balfour's lack of decisiveness and faulty political judgement must bear a heavy share of the responsibility for the Liberal victory.

A Chamberlain Opens the Campaign

Well, you see the point. You want an Empire. Do you think it better to cultivate the trade with your own people or let that go in order that you may keep the trade of those who, rightly enough, are your competitors and rivals? I say it is a new position. I say the people of this Empire have got to consider it. I do not want to hasten that decision. They have two alternatives before them. They may maintain if they like the interpretation, in my mind an entirely artificial and wrong interpretation, which has been placed upon the doctrines of free trade by a small remnant of Little Englanders of the Manchester School who now profess to be the sole repositories of the doctrines of Mr Cobden and Mr Bright. They may maintain that policy in all its severity, although it is repudiated by every other nation and by all your colonies. In that case they will be absolutely precluded from giving any kind of preference or favour to any of their colonies abroad, or even protecting their colonies abroad when they offer favour to us. This is the first alternative. The second alternative is that we should insist we will not be bound by any purely technical definition of free trade, that, while we seek as one chief object free interchange of trade and commerce between ourselves and all the nations of the world, we will nevertheless recover our freedom, resume that power of negotiation, and if necessary, retaliate whenever our own interests or our relations between our colonies and ourselves are threatened by other people. I leave the matter in your hands. I desire that a discussion on this subject should be opened. The time has not yet come to settle it; but it seems to me that for good or evil this is an issue much greater in its consequences than any of our local disputes. Make a mistake in your legislation, yet it can be corrected; make a mistake in your Imperial policy, it is irretrievable.

From Chamberlain's speech at Birmingham, 15 May 1903

B Balfour's View on the Tariff Reform Question

Fiscal reform is, and must remain, the first constructive work of the Unionist party; its objects are to secure more equal terms of competition for British trade and closer commercial union with the colonies; and while it is at present unnecessary to prescribe the exact methods by which these objects are to be attained, and inexpedient to permit differences of opinion as to these methods to divide the party, though other means are possible, the establishment of a moderate general tariff on manufactured goods not imposed for the purpose of raising prices or giving artificial protection against legitimate competition and the imposition of a small duty on foreign corn are not in principle objectionable and should be adopted if shown to be necessary for the attainment of the ends in view or for the purpose of revenue.

From a letter by Balfour, February 1906

C A Liberal View of Balfour's Resignation

By December 1905 there was every reason for taking the opinion of the electors. For ten years there had been no General Election except that of 1900, which had been taken in the middle of the South African War, and was therefore no opportunity for the expression of popular opinion on anything else except the war. Tariff Reform was a new issue; it had now been debated before the country for over two years. It was therefore altogether reasonable, right, and proper that there should now be a Dissolution and a General Election. But there was no apparent reason why Mr Balfour's government should have resigned: they had a good majority in parliament; it was more than two years since the Free Trade members of the Government had resigned; the shock of that had not broken up the government then and could not be the cause of its resignation now. The only conceivable reason was that the government were exhausted and tired – not a good recommendation for giving them support at the polls. There is no doubt that this resignation was a great tactical disadvantage to them.

From Earl Grey of Fallodon (foreign secretary 1905–16): *Twenty-Five Years* (1925)

D An Historian's Comment on the Results of the 1906 General Election

The overturn, which took everyone by surprise, was significant of a greater tendency to mass emotion in the large modern electorate, bred in great cities, and less tied up by party traditions than the old. There have been other such elections since. Moreover the issues of 1906 had all been unfavourable to the late government – the Education Act, Protection, Taff Vale, and the recent introduction of indentured Chinese labour into the South African gold mines, which seemed a sorry outcome of the great Imperialist War. But behind all these things was something more fundamental. A new generation had arisen, wanting new things and caring more about 'social reform' at home than about 'Imperialism' in Ireland, South Africa or anywhere else.

From G.M. Trevelyan: *History of England* (1927)

Questions

1 Assess Chamberlain's tactics and political skills as shown in Source A.

(6 marks)

2 How far does Balfour's letter (Source B) show that he had been won over by 1906 to support tariff reform? **(6 marks)**

3 Using your own knowledge and Source C, consider the value to historians of Earl Grey's views. **(5 marks)**

4 How far do sources C and D agree on the importance of the tariff reform issue in the 1906 General Election? **(6 marks)**

5 Using your own knowledge and the sources, consider to what extent these sources provide an adequate explanation of Conservative weakness in 1906. **(7 marks)**

2 LIBERALISM TRIUMPHANT

1906-9

The electoral success of 1906 gave the Liberal Party a sizeable majority over all other parties. The Conservative Party had its number of MPs reduced by more than a half, while the Labour Party had some success but had not yet made significant inroads in traditional working-class areas – even at Merthyr Tydfil the Liberal topped the poll. Moreover, the Liberals could count on general support from both the Labour Party and the Irish Nationalists; the Conservatives were isolated by the combined political forces of their traditional enemies.

Ironically, successful Conservative strong-arm tactics in Ireland had drastically reduced Irish violence, and Conservative land reform had bought off some of the peasantry. Thus the Irish Question which had so divided the Liberals in Gladstone's day seemed no longer so urgent, and such was the size of the Liberal majority that it was unnecessary for the Liberals to promise Home Rule in return for the Nationalists' parliamentary support.

The Liberals therefore could choose their own legislative programme. The old tug-of-war between *laisser-faire* liberalism and interventionist liberalism was over. Lloyd George and the radical wing were to be given what they wanted, and the election promises of 1906 were to be fulfilled. Thus the Trade Disputes Act, legislation for the protection of children and shop workers, factory conditions, education and old age pensions were the product of the new, vital liberalism, and the curtain-raisers in what was expected to be a long and continued process of reform. With hindsight the period can be identified as the last flowering of liberalism, but it did not seem so at the time. To contemporaries it seemed inevitable that the 1906 electoral triumph of the Liberals would be repeated, that the Conservatives had lost the working-class vote, that Labour would never gain it, and that continued Liberal triumphs were inevitable. Until 1909 there was hardly a cloud on the Liberal horizon, apart from the irritating habit of the House of Lords in interfering with some, but by no means all, of the Liberal legislation. The Liberal Party had to meet the Lords' challenge, but perhaps was not expecting so stiff a fight.

A Lloyd George's Reply When Asked About Old Age Pensions During the Election of 1906

As to old-age pensions. The money spent on the South African War would have been sufficient to give old-age pensions to every man over 65. They had reckoned it up at the time. They also discussed the question of 60 or 65 years of age, and they found that the difference between the two limits meant about twelve to twenty millions. At the present time it would be impossible to get the people of this country to face an expenditure or twenty million pounds on anything. Therefore the matter, when taken up, must be taken up gradually. They must, first of all, put the national finances in spick and span order, and then see that every man too old to pursue his ordinary avocation [employment] should be saved from the humiliation of workhouse or parish charity.

From a speech at Caernarvon, 19 January 1906

B Lloyd George's Wider View, June 1908

You have never had a scheme of this kind tried in a great country klike ours, with its thronging millions, with its rooted complexities; and everyone who has been engaged in any kind of reform knows how difficult it is to make way through the inextricable tangle of an old society like ours. This is, therefore, a great experiment . . . We do not say that it deals with all the problems of unmerited destitution in this country. We do not even contend that it deals with the worst part of that problem. It might be held that many an old man dependent on the charity of the parish was better off than many a young man, broken down in health, or who cannot find a market for his labour. The provision which is made for the sick and unemployed is grossly inadequate in this country, and yet the working-classes have done their best during 50 years to make provision without the aid of the State. But it is insufficient. The old man has to bear his own burden, while in the case of a young man, who is broken down and who has a wife and family to maintain, the suffering is increased and multiplied to that extent. These problems of the sick, of the infirm, of the men who cannot find means of earning a livelihood are problems with which it is the business of the State to deal; they are problems which the State has neglected too long.

From a speech in Parliament, 15 June 1908

C A Contemporary View of Lloyd George

THE PHILANTHROPIC HIGHWAYMAN.

Mr. Lloyd-George. *"I'LL MAKE 'EM PITY THE AGED POOR!"*

From *Punch*, 5 August 1908

D A Protest against Universal Pensions

Sir,

. . . However the Ministers may attempt to hide it, we are in fact in the presence of the universal out-door relief scheme divested of the restraining provisions of the present Poor Law. How can any prudent man contemplate such a situation without dismay? The strength of this kingdom, in all its past struggles, has been its great reserve of wealth and the sturdy independent character of its people. The measure which is being pushed through the House of Commons with haste and acclaim will destroy both sources. It will extort the wealth from its possessors by unjust taxation. It will distribute it in small doles, the most wasteful of all forms of expenditure, and will sap the character of the people by teaching them to rely, not on their own exertions, but on the State.

From C.H.T. Crosthwaite's letter to *The Times*, 3 July 1908

E Those Entitled to Benefit Under the Old Age Pensions Act

. . . 2 The statutory conditions for the receipt of an old age pension by any person are:

(a) The person must have attained the age of seventy.
(b) The person must satisfy the pension authorities that for at least twenty years up to the date of the receipt of any sum on account of a pension he has been a British subject, and has had his residence, as defined by regulations under this Act, in the United Kingdom.
(c) The person must satisfy the pension authorities that his yearly means as calculated under this Act do not exceed thirty-one pounds ten shillings.

3(a) A person shall be disqualified from receiving or continuing to receive an old age pension under this Act notwithstanding the fulfilment of the statutory conditions:
  (i) While he is in receipt of any poor relief . . .
  (ii) If, before he becomes entitled to a pension, he has habitually failed to work according to his ability, opportunity, and need, for the maintenance or benefit of himself and those legally dependent on him . . .
  (iii) While he is detained in any asylum within the meaning of the Lunacy Act, 1890, or while he is being maintained in any place as a pauper or criminal lunatic . . .
  (iv) During the continuance of any period of disqualification arising or imposed in pursuance of this section in consequence of conviction for an offence.
(b) . . . While he is detained in prison . . . and for a further period of ten years after the date on which he is released from prison.
(c) Where a person of sixty years of age or upwards having been

convicted before any court is liable to have a detention order made against him under the Inebriates Act, 1898, and is not necessarily, by virtue of the provisions of this Act, disqualified for receiving or continuing to receive an old age pension under this Act, the court may, if they think fit, order that the person so convicted be so disqualified for such a period, not exceeding ten years, as the Court direct.

From An Act to Provide for Old Age Pensions, 1 August 1908

Questions

1 To what extent do Sources A and B show a change in attitude towards pensions on Lloyd George's part between 1906 and 1908? **(5 marks)**

2 Compare the point of view of the cartoonist in Source C with that of the author of the letter in Source D. **(7 marks)**

3 Using your own knowledge, explain 'the restraining provisions of the present Poor Law' referred to in Source D. **(4 marks)**

4 'The restrictive provisions of the Act in Source E tells us more about contemporary society than about contemporary attempts at economy'. How far do you agree? **(6 marks)**

5 Using the sources and your own knowledge, assess the motives of the government in introducing old age pensions. **(8 marks)**

3 LIBERALISM IN CRISIS
1909–14

Despite their achievements in the years to 1909, the Liberals never enjoyed a real honeymoon period in office. It is true that they possessed a huge and unchallengeable majority in the House of Commons, that the Irish Question could be safely ignored, and that Labour appeared to pose no serious threat to liberalism's claim to the moral high ground of radicalism. But the House of Lords had tampered with the Liberal legislative programme, provoking an untypical outburst from Campbell-Bannerman in 1907, and making inevitable the head-on conflict which Gladstone had prophesied in 1894. Meanwhile, slowly rising prices and the Trade Disputes Act of 1906 had given trade unions the motive and the means to threaten and carry out strikes in increasing numbers, and the suffragettes supplied the women's political movement with the militancy which the suffragists had lacked.

These domestic problems did not seem serious enough to deflect the government from its battle with the Lords. Lloyd George's budget of 1909 could have found other, less controversial ways of raising the necessary revenue, and his intemperate language in defence of his budget has been seen by many as a deliberate attempt to provoke the Lords. However, the two general elections of 1910 deprived the Liberals of their absolute majority and forced Liberal dependence on Irish and Labour votes. 'Commons v. Lords' was not the election rallying cry that many Liberals had hoped it would be. The long drawn-out crisis did lead to restrictions on the power of the Lords, though not to the intended major reform of its membership. The Parliament Act asserted in legislation what had long been accepted in practice: the superiority of the lower House of Parliament. But it deprived the House of Lords of its power to fight long rear-guard actions against any legislation it might arbitrarily choose to dislike.

The constitutional crisis revived the Irish Question. Demand for Home Rule had never died away, although land reform under Wyndham had reduced agrarian discontent. However, in 1910–11 the Irish Nationalists held the balance of political power, and the price demanded by them for their support in curbing the Lords was a Home Rule Bill. This led to Ulster's Solemn League and Covenant, the raising of rival armies, gun-running, violence, the near treason of Conservative leaders such as Sir Edward Carson, and the so-called Curragh Mutiny of 1914. The government's preoccupation with the House of Lords, Ireland, and the growing militancy of the trade unions brought frustration to the suffragettes and led to their increasing use of violence, hunger strikes and the Cat and Mouse Act. Syndicalism and adverse economic conditions increased trade union activity, and the strikes which followed on the railways and in the mines in 1912 were symptomatic of widespread industrial discontent. It has been argued that the Liberals dealt effectively with the Lords crisis, but that Asquith was irresolute in his handling of Ireland, undecided on whether to use strong-arm tactics in dealing with the trade unions, and heavy-handed and unfeeling in his attitude towards the suffragettes. Some see weaknesses in his leadership in these years as a prelude to his alleged incompetence in war which led to his replacement by Lloyd George in 1916.

Yet it must not be forgotten that, despite all the domestic turmoil of these crisis years, and despite the distractions of managing an effective foreign policy in the face of a series of international crises, the Liberal government was tackling health and unemployment insurance, even if other areas of its previous reforming zeal received less attention. The crisis of 1909–11 did not absolutely distract the Liberal government from reform. The insurance and health legislation of 1911 can be regarded as more far-reaching than any of its work from 1906–9. The foundations of the welfare state were laid by a government exhausted from a constitutional conflict, beset by labour troubles, harassed by suffragettes, committed to a bruising contest on Ireland, and moreover without the comfortable majority of 1906. There seemed much life in the Liberal Party yet. Dangerfield, in his *The Strange Death of Liberal England* (1936), attributes the ensuing rapid decline of Liberalism to the crises of 1909–14. But these crises were, in the main, being effectively handled, and modern writers see 1914–18 as the crisis period for the Liberals.

A Budget Demonstration in London, 24 July 1909

The great demonstration at Hyde Park, London, on Saturday, in favour of the land clauses of the Budget, received enthusiastic support from all parts of the country, and it is estimated that 250,000 Liberals gathered round the platform.

The procession from the Thames Embankment to Hyde Park took about an hour to pass through Trafalgar Square, where the traffic got badly 'hung up'. Some of the marchers were suburbanly smart, and there was an occasional silk hat, while other contingents had the appearance of the unemployed. The trade unionists, with their painted silk banners flapping in the breeze, made the best show.

The resolution forming the text for the speakers was, 'That this meeting heartily welcomes the important provisions contained in the Budget for taxing monopolists and socially created wealth, and particularly for securing a complete valuation of all land in the United Kingdom, holding this to be essential to any policy of land and social reform'.

It further hoped that 'the Government will firmly resist any mutilation of their proposals dictated by selfish interests, and will seek an early opportunity for so extending them as to secure the best use of the land, which must result in increased employment, better housing for the people, and greater prosperity for our national industries'.

It was a bad day for the banner-bearers, owing to the stiff wind, and the flagmen who had fixed their colours to wagonettes or antique omnibuses had the best time of it. 'Cobden stood for free land.' 'Tax land, not food.' 'Shall those who own the land rule the people? No!' 'The Budget must be law.' 'Tax the idlers – not the workers.' 'Right, not robbery.' 'Land for the landless' and 'Hurrah for Lloyd George' were a few of the mottoes displayed.

During the afternoon some seventy contingents with about eight bands arrived on the Thames Embankment from all parts of the Metropolis – a fine piece of organisation by the Budget League.

From the *Northern Echo*, 26 July 1909

B Lloyd George Defends the Budget

The other day, at the great Tory meeting held at the Cannon-Street Hotel, they had blazoned on the walls, 'We protest against the Budget in the name of democracy, liberty and justice.' Where does democracy come in this landed system? Where is the justice in all these transactions? We claim that the tax we impose is fair, just and moderate. They go on threatening that if we proceed they will cut down their benefactions and discharge labour. What kind of labour? What is the labour they are going to choose for dismissal? . . . Are they going to reduce their gamekeepers? That would be sad. The agricultural labourer and the farmer might then have some part of the game which they fatten with their labour. But what would happen to you in the season? No week-end shooting with the Duke of Norfolk for any of us. But that is not the kind of labour they are going to cut down. They are going to cut down productive labour – builders and gardeners – and they are going to ruin their property so that it shall not be taxed . . .

But I do not believe it. They have threatened and menaced like that before. They have seen that it is not in their interest to carry out these futile menaces. They are now protesting against paying their fair share of the taxation of land and they are doing so by saying: 'You are burdening the community; you are putting burdens upon the people which they cannot bear'. Ah! They are not thinking of themselves. Noble souls! It is not the grand dukes they are feeling for, it is the market gardener, the builder, and it was, until recently, the smallholder. In every debate in the House of Commons they said: 'We are not worrying for ourselves. We can afford it with our broad acres; but just think of the little man who has only got a few acres'; and we were so very impressed with this tearful appeal that at last we said, 'We will leave him out' and I almost expected to see Mr Pretyman [an important Conservative MP] jump over the table and say: 'Fall on my neck and embrace me'. Instead of that, he stiffened up, his face wreathed with anger, and he said, 'The Budget is more unjust than ever'.

From Lloyd George's speech at Limehouse, 30 July 1909

C Asquith Attacks the Lords' Rejection of the Budget

The truth is that all this talk about the duty or right of the House of Lords to refer measures to the people is, in the light of our practical and actual experience, the hollowest outcry of political cant. We never hear of it, as I pointed out, when a Tory government is in power. It is never suggested when measures are thrust by a Tory majority by the aid of the guillotine and the Closure, and all the rest of it, through this House – measures which, unlike every one of the governing provisions of the Budget of the present year, have never been approved or even submitted to the electorate. It is simply a thin rhetorical veneer, by which it is sought to gloss over the partisan, and in this case the unconstitutional, action of the purely partisan Chamber. The sum and substance of the matter is that the House of Lords rejected the Finance Bill last Tuesday, not because they love the people, but because they hate the Budget. This motion, which I am now about to propose is confined in terms to the new and unprecedented claim made by the House of Lords to interfere in finance. But I am sure, in fact I know, I am speaking the minds of my colleagues, and, I believe, of the great bulk of those who are sitting on this side of the House, when I say that it represents a stage – a momentous and perhaps decisive stage – in a protracted controversy which is drawing to a close. The real question which emerges from the political struggles in this country for the last thirty years is not whether you will have a single or double chamber system of government, but whether when the Tory Party is in power the House of Commons shall be omnipotent, and whether when the Liberal Party is in power the House of Lords shall be omnipotent.

From Asquith's Speech in the Commons, 2 December 1909

D An Historian's View

Neither in form nor substance was it an ordinary Budget. The dark threats that preceded it; the method and manner of its introduction; the place accorded to it in the legislative work of the Session; the wide range of its proposals; the almost insoluble complexity of its details; the vagueness of its financial forecasts – all combined to give it an exceptional, indeed an unprecedented character. Mr Lloyd George bettered the example set by Mr Gladstone in 1861. He combined into one conglomerate Bill not only all the tax Bills of the year, but virtually all the legislative proposals of the Session, not to say all the rejected proposals of an entire parliament . . .

The Minister made no concealment of the purpose underlying his proposals. 'This' he said, is a war budget. It is for raising money to wage implacable war against poverty and squalidness.' . . .

The fiscal [tax] value of these proposals was evidently prospective, not immediate. Their yield for the current year was estimated by the Minister at no more than half a million. 'An amount', he added with grim humour, 'which must not be regarded as any indication of the revenue they will ultimately produce.'

From J.A.R. Marriott: *Modern England, 1885–1945* (third edition 1946)

E Financial Return from the New Duties on Land
Revenue produced by the 1909 Land Duties, 1909–1919, £1,087,440.
Cost of collection of the duties and the accompanying land valuation, 1909–1919, £4,600,000.

Adapted from Marriott, *ibid*.

Questions

1 (i) Using your own knowledge, explain the references to the 'mottoes' in Source A (lines 23–6). **(3 marks)**

  (ii) What are the uses and limitations of Source A to an historian investigating the Budget Crisis? **(4 marks)**

2 How far does Source B support the view that the House of Lords was provoked by Lloyd George into opposing the Budget? **(6 marks)**

3 Compare the techniques used by the speakers in Sources B and C to convey an effective message. **(5 marks)**

4 'Historians should give a balanced view.' How impartial do you consider Marriott to be? **(6 marks)**

5 How far do these sources suggest that the House of Lords would be unwise to oppose the Budget? **(6 marks)**

4 THE IMPACT OF WAR UPON POLITICS 1914–18

Britain's entry into the war in 1914 caused much heart-searching among Liberals, and there were several ministerial resignations. Total war, although its onset was gradual, was alien to the spirit of liberalism in that it implied central state intervention and compulsion, ideas from which many Liberals, including Asquith, recoiled. Thus there was from the beginning of the war an impression of half-heartedness, muddle and hand-to-mouth management which gave rise to dissatisfaction in the press and among the informed populace, and frustration among those ministers like Churchill and Lloyd George who wanted more vigour and leadership in the conduct of the war. When, in May 1915, Asquith agreed to the formation of a coalition government, his position was weakened rather than strengthened: those of the government who wanted to pursue the war most vigorously were either from Conservative ranks, or maverick Liberals. Of these the most prominent was Lloyd George, who put his anti-war sentiment of 1900 behind him in recognising, as he saw it, the justice and necessity of the war against Germany, and the need to pursue it single-mindedly.

Liberals were much troubled by the issue of conscription. Threats of resignation by Lloyd George and others unless it were adopted forced it upon a divided Cabinet. Asquith then took advantage of a closing of patriotic ranks over the Easter Rebellion to persuade Parliament to finalise it largely shorn of the exemptions and exceptions which had previously salved Liberal consciences. But conscription was not enough. The accumulated failures of the war continued to be laid at the door of the government. Lloyd George's frustration at being unable to secure rapid decisions on matters of vital importance led him to propose a War Committee from which the Prime Minister would, in effect, be virtually excluded. It would, Lloyd George believed, run the war decisively. His motives appeared to many to be genuine and patriotic, but to others, especially those Liberals who had been suspicious of conscription and of his methods to secure it, Lloyd George seemed politically ambitious and untrustworthy in his disloyalty. He had long been suspected of using allies in the press in order to advance his own interests.

Thus cornered by Lloyd George, Asquith at first agreed to the proposed War Committee and his own very restricted role in it. Yet immediately after, angered by a supposed press leak by Lloyd George and urged on by Lloyd George's enemies within and outside the Cabinet, Asquith went back on his promise. Lloyd George felt bound to resign, but Asquith seemed unprepared for the attitude of the Conservatives in the Coalition who supported Lloyd George. Their resignations made Asquith's position untenable, and Lloyd George took office as prime minister.

To many historians, this obscure and unnecessary squabble had momentous importance. The refusal of the Liberal ministers to serve under Lloyd George meant that he conducted the war with the support of the Conservatives and some of the rank-and-file Liberal radicals. However, the traditional base of the Liberal Party, including its most senior leaders, was now ranged against him in opposition. Admittedly Asquith promised to support the new government, yet he and his followers did in fact take on the role of official opposition. Perhaps Asquith intended this to be formal only, but the Liberal split was widened by the Maurice debate. Here an argument over whether British front-line troops in France were stronger in January 1918 than in January 1917 led to recriminations, accusations of government dishonesty, and to the Asquith opposition actually dividing the House and voting against the government in May 1918.

It was not surprising that at the general election seven months later, the Asquith Liberals fought the Coalition government and were humiliatingly defeated. The beneficiaries were the Conservatives who fought for Lloyd George and the Coalition, and who now provided by far the largest political group amongst Lloyd George's supporters. Without a strong radical element the Asquith Liberals seemed like a negative party; a brief revival in 1923 was due more to their opposition to tariff reform than to any positive programme. Reconciliation between the two Liberal leaders, such as that in 1923, was always insecure and temporary, and the Liberal split remained a constant factor preventing Liberal revival and precipitating the long Liberal decline.

A Proposed Reconstruction of the War Committee

1. That the War Committee consist of three members – two of whom must be the First Lord of the Admiralty and the Secretary of State for War, who shall have in their offices deputies capable of attending to and deciding all departmental business, and a third minister without portfolio. One of the three to be Chairman.
2. That the War Committee shall have full powers, subject to the supreme control of the Prime Minister, to direct all questions connected with the war.
3. The Prime Minister in his discretion to have the power to refer any question to the Cabinet.
4. Unless the Cabinet on reference by the Prime Minister reverses the decision of the War Committee, that decision to be carried out by the Department concerned.

5. The War Committee to have power to invite any Minister, and to summon the expert advisers and officers of any Department to its meetings.

Memorandum drawn up by Bonar Law, Carson, Aitken and Lloyd George and presented to Asquith on 1 December 1916

B Asquith's Initial Reaction to the Memorandum
My dear Lloyd George,

I have now had time to reflect on our conversation this morning and to study your memorandum.

Though I do not altogether share your dark estimate and forecast of the situation, actual and prospective, I am in complete agreement that we have reached a critical situation in the War, and that our methods of procedure, with the experience that we have gained during the last three months, call for reconsideration and revision.

The two main defects of the War Council, which has done excellent work, are (1) that its numbers are too large, and (2) that there is delay, evasion, and often obstruction on the part of the Departments in giving effect to its decisions.

I might with good reason add (3) that it is often kept in ignorance by the Departments of information, essential and even vital, of a technical kind, upon the problems that come before it; and (4) that it is overcharged with duties, many of which might well be delegated to subordinate bodies . . .

In my opinion, whatever changes are made in the composition or functions of the War Council the Prime Minister must be its Chairman. He cannot be relegated to the position of an arbiter in the background or a referee in the Cabinet . . .

I purposely in this letter do not discuss the delicate and difficult question of personnel.

From Asquith's letter to Lloyd George, 1 December 1916

C Interpretation of the Verbal Agreement Between Asquith and Lloyd George
The suggested arrangement [of the previous day] was to the following effect: The Prime Minister to have supreme and effective control of war policy. The agenda of the War Committee will be submitted to him daily; he can direct it to consider particular topics or proposals; and all its conclusions will be subject to his approval or veto. He can, of course, at his own discretion attend meetings of the Committee.

From Asquith's letter to Lloyd George, 4 December 1916

D Asquith's Second Thoughts

My dear Lloyd George,

Thank you for your letter of this morning. The King gave me authority today to ask and accept the resignation of all my colleagues, and to form a new government on such lines as I shall submit to him.

I start therefore with a clean slate.

The first question I have to consider is the constitution of the new War Committee.

After full consideration of this matter in all its aspects, I have come decidedly to the conclusion that it is not possible that such a Committee could be made workable and effective without the Prime Minister as its Chairman. I quite agree that it will be necessary for him, in view of the other calls on his time and energy, to delegate from time to time the Chairmanship to another Minister as his representative . . . but, if he is to retain the authority which corresponds to his responsibility as Prime Minister he must continue to be, as he has always been, its permanent President. I am satisfied on reflection that any other arrangement, e.g. the one I indicated to you in my letter of today, would be in experience impracticable and incompatible with the Prime Minister's final and supreme control. The other question you have raised relates to the personnel of the Committee. Here again after deliberate consideration I find myself unable to agree with some of your suggestions.

From Asquith to Lloyd George, 4 December 1916

E Lloyd George's Resignation

As all delay is fatal in war, I place my office without further parley at your disposal.

It is with great personal regret that I have come to this conclusion. In spite of mean and unworthy insinuations to the contrary – insinuations which I fear are always inevitable in the case of men who hold prominent but not primary positions in any administration – I have felt a strong personal attachment to you as my chief. As you yourself said, on Sunday, we have acted together for ten years and never had a quarrel, although we have had many grave differences on questions of policy. You have treated me with great courtesy and kindness; for all that I thank you. Nothing would have induced me to part now except an overwhelming sense that the course of action which has been pursued has put the country – and not merely the country, but throughout the world, the principles for which you and I have always stood throughout our political lives – in the greatest peril that has ever overtaken them.

As I am fully conscious of the importance of preserving national unity, I propose to give your Government complete support in the vigorous prosecution of the War; but unity without action is nothing but futile carnage, and I cannot be responsible for that. Vigour and Vision are the supreme need at this hour.

Lloyd George to Asquith, 5 December 1916

F Sir Edward Grey's Comment on the Affair
A friend has reminded me that one day, as we came away from a War Council, late in November or early in December 1916, I said to him, commenting on what had passed there, 'Lloyd George means to break up the Government'. This happened in no long time. Lloyd George forced a crisis by resigning; the Liberal members of the Government held a separate meeting with Asquith to decide what course should be taken. The opinion in favour of resignation was unanimous. Whether we were all of the same opinion for the same reason I cannot say. My own view was clear; the present position was very unsatisfactory; people were not working well together, and the Government was not receiving from the country the confidence and support that were essential to make it efficient. The only thing to be done was for the Government to clear up the situation by resigning.

From Early Grey of Fallodon: *Twenty-Five Years* (1925)

Questions

1 a) What can be deduced from Sources A and B about the defects of the old War Council? **(6 marks)**

   a) From your own knowledge, how far would you agree with Asquith's comment in December 1916 (Source B) that 'we have reached a critical situation in the war'? **(10 marks)**

2 'Sources C and D show that Asquith's error was not in going back on his word, but in agreeing to Lloyd George's proposals against his better judgement.' How far do you agree? **(6 marks)**

3 Do Sources A–E support Grey's view (Source F) of Lloyd George's motives in this crisis? **(6 marks)**

4 It was known by the authors of letters B–E that publication was probable. What reservations have you about accepting such letters at face value? **(5 marks)**

5 Using the sources and your own knowledge, consider whether Asquith or Lloyd George was more to blame for the fall of Asquith's government. **(7 marks)**

5 THE IMPACT OF WAR ON SOCIETY 1914–18

The South African War had made little impact on the lives of the British people. Those who had menfolk in the volunteer regular army might travel to Southampton to give the troops a patriotic send-off, and later peruse the casualty lists with dread. Others might be glum at bad news, and rejoice at the lifting of sieges such as Mafeking. But life continued as normal: food prices remained constant, there were no shortages, and no civilian life was placed directly in danger by the war.

There is a temptation to point up the contrast with the First World War. Between 1914 and 1918 most fit young men were sent to France, so that the war directly touched nearly every family. Women were encouraged to take up employment to fill the gaps left by military recruitment. State direction and State regulation, especially through the all-embracing Defence of the Realm Act, impinged on many aspects of daily life. Food scarcities occurred and food rationing was introduced, either to cope with shortages or to allay unnecessary fear of them. Prices more than doubled, although wages rose at a faster rate. German naval bombardment of the coasts caused some casualties among civilians; Zeppelin raids and hand-bombing from aircraft killed nearly 1500. Nevertheless, these inconveniences were regarded as temporary, and as far as possible life continued much as before.

Perhaps the war accelerated social trends that were already in evidence in 1914. The emancipation and enfranchisement of women moved a little faster after the war when the absence of suffragette militancy encouraged politicians to be less defensive, but the limited female suffrage of 1918 can hardly be regarded as a direct reward for women's contribution to the war. Almost all the jobs made available to women during the war were denied to them after the war ended. Conversely, the decline of domestic service, or rather the increasing difficulty experienced by stately homes after 1918 in recruiting adequate and suitable staff, was at least in part due to growing employment prospects for women. However, this had more to do with the growth of service industries than the impact of war.

The war did encourage some fringe erosion of class barriers, it greatly broadened the base of taxation, and it accelerated Britain's industrial and commercial decline. Indeed, many historians have argued that the social effects of the First World War were mainly temporary, that its political effects were more far-reaching, and that its economic effects were the most permanent.

A The Immediate Problems of War

Let us think first of the poor. During the week-end there were the beginnings of a panic with reference to the supplies of food. Dealers in some towns were almost swept bare. Only when the shops were closed for the holidays, and provisions were not obtainable, did the poorest begin to fear for their supply of bread. Were it not for the steps taken yesterday by Parliament, we might have seen the panic develop to its height. We may now hope to see some of the anxiety lessened by the announcement of the provisions made for keeping up the flow of food into the country. With the corn in hand and the harvest being reaped we have supplies equal to our needs up to Christmas. But means are being adopted to enable our importers to receive supplies from America and Canada. The Government have stepped in to accept eighty per cent of the risk to cargoes, so that shipping firms may not hesitate to carry on their business, and so that the price of food shall not be increased too seriously because of the cost of importation. As this applies to materials essential to our manufacturers, there is a reduction to the risk of our industries being stopped for want of them.

Editorial from the *Northern Echo*, 5 August 1914

B Modification of the Potato Regulation

From November 19 the minimum potato price of £6 per ton to the grower is to be abolished. A free market is to be allowed for sales by growers throughout the kingdom, subject to the continuance of the existing maximum price of £6.10s. per ton . . .

The changes to be made to meet the altered conditions have come about since Lord Devonport fixed the minimum price at the beginning of the year. At that time there was a great shortage of potatoes, together with high prices and uncertainty for the future. The minimum price was designed to ensure a big production, and £6 was fixed upon as fairly representing the cost of production . . . in order to guarantee the farmer against loss.

It has now been discovered that farmers in some districts, notably in Scotland and in Northern Ireland, where there has been an abnormally large crop of potatoes coupled with acute transport difficulties, are willing to sell their potatoes at less than the £6 minimum in order to get rid of their crops. The new policy is designed chiefly to meet this situation. It allows the free play of the market while maintaining the present maximum, but in order that the Government may keep its pledge to the grower the State will subsidise the farmer against losses arising from the abolition of the minimum. In practice, therefore, the minimum is retained, with the difference that the price is made up to the farmer by a Government subsidy.

This is in effect an extension of the policy of the bread subsidy to potatoes.

From the *Manchester Guardian*, 9 November 1917

C Cotton Supplies

The seriousness of the cotton position in Lancashire is shown in the result of the census recently taken by the Cotton Control Board and now published with the approval of the Government. Since the figures were compiled matters have become worse still, as the November shipments will only amount to about ten days' consumption, and no forecast of the December shipments can yet be made . . .

Although stocks of cotton are low compared with pre-war days, no trouble would be anticipated if the cotton ships were reaching this country regularly with moderate consignments of cotton. A simple calculation will show that there is only sufficient cotton available to keep the mills running until the end of the year. According to the Liverpool Cotton Association's circular the cotton at sea amounts to 203,000 bales, barely enough to keep the mills running another month. But the industry would not be wise to count cotton at sea as if it were landed. Assuming that all the cotton at sea is landed and the Shipping Controller adheres to his policy of reducing the transport of cotton, the crisis will have become acute before Christmas.

From the *Manchester Guardian*, 16 November 1917

D Daylight Saving

The Government may pass fifty Daylight Saving Bills, but I for one shall certainly not alter my watches and clocks to play the childish game of 'let's pretend'. Neither will the man who generally goes to bed at ten o'clock retire at nine just because his watch is an hour fast. The proposal of a humorist that a Bill should be introduced to raise the thermometer 20 degrees in the winter and lower it 20 degrees in the summer is just as sensible.

From a letter to the *Daily Mirror*, May 1916

E Rationing

The food position [in 1917] was in fact better than it had been earlier in the year. The wheat harvest of 1917 was the best of the century. Supplies of meat and fat were coming in faster. Yet, without warning, people everywhere took alarm and bought food irrationally. There were disappointed queues at every butcher's and grocer's shop. The Ministry of Food had to introduce rationing helter-skelter early in 1918, not at all because food was scarce, but simply to allay this strange disturbance. There was no intention of reducing the consumption of food. The ration book was a promise that all demands would be met, as indeed they were, and, since people took up their full ration, consumption slightly increased. This was war psychology at its most mysterious.

From A.J.P. Taylor: *English History, 1914–1945*

F Statistics on the War Period

	£m value		1914 = 100	
	imports	exports	gross national product	prices
1914	700	530	100	100
1915	860	480	103	130
1916	940	600	96	145
1917	1060	590	90	190
1918	1250	540	87	220

Adapted from various sources

Questions

1 What do you consider to have been the main aim of the editorial in Source A? **(4 marks)**

2 Why do you think that the government was willing to allow the alarmist report of the Cotton Control Board (Source C) to be published? **(4 marks)**

3 From your own knowledge and from your study of source E, consider how accurate is the impression given by A.J.P. Taylor of the circumstances which led to food rationing. **(5 marks)**

4 What evidence is there in these sources of the difficulties faced by the government in trying to regulate the wartime food supply? **(7 marks)**

5 Are statistics such as Source F the most reliable type of source? **(5 marks)**

6 'The government had no coherent policy for regulating the economy during the war. It developed one by accident.' Using the sources and your own knowledge, show how far you would agree with this judgement. **(10 marks)**

6 LLOYD GEORGE, LEADER WITHOUT A PARTY 1918–22

The enormous majority (229) which the electorate had given to the Coalition government in the general election of 1918 appeared to be a vote of confidence for Lloyd George. It seemed to him to be a clear mandate for him to tackle domestic problems, foreign affairs and Ireland in whatever ways seemed to him the best. And this without the tiresome irritant of a Conservative opposition similar to that which had hounded him in Parliament in the last years before the war. That 339 of his supporters were Conservatives or Unionists did not dismay him; they had secured their election under the protection of his coupon, and they owed their election to Lloyd George's name, not to Conservative policies.

However, this did not necessarily seem the case to a number of Conservatives. If 339 MPs had secured election under the Conservative banner, by far the largest party in the House, why was there not a Conservative prime minister? Perhaps all agreed in 1918 with the need for national unity and reconstruction. But Lloyd George's personal domination of the Cabinet, his riding rough-shod over colleagues such as Lord Curzon, his tortuous Irish policy, the Honours' Scandal, and finally the Chanak Crisis caused increasing uneasiness and alarm within the Conservative ranks. Some Scottish Conservatives felt that their majorities depended on Lloyd George's name, but many believed that he depended more on the Conservatives than they did on him. After all, where could he go? The Asquith Liberals were alienated beyond reconciliation. His heavy-handed treatment of Henderson in 1917 meant that the Labour Party was going its own way and was unlikely to support him – despite their common radicalism. Thus Lloyd George, the radical, was not the leader of a left-wing party, but the head of a right-wing party whose own leadership was submissive to him, but whose rank and file was becoming increasingly restless.

As discontent mounted in 1922, Austen Chamberlain, the Conservative leader, and his more senior colleagues saw their political future in a general election to renew the Coalition under Lloyd George's dynamic leadership. Junior Conservative ministers and many rank-and-file Conservative MPs became alarmed. Disaster threatened the Conservative Party either way: if it remained loyal to Lloyd George it would lose its Conservative identity, even if it managed to retain its unity; if it was to disown Lloyd George a party split seemed inevitable.

In this situation the conduct of Baldwin is crucial; that of Bonar Law probably even more so. Baldwin's apologists claim that his motives in turning against Lloyd George were sincere, and that he fully expected to be worsted by a triumphant Lloyd George and driven from public life; others see Baldwin as devious, and determined on self-advancement which could only be achieved if Lloyd George were removed from his path. As for Bonar Law's emergence from retirement, was it forced on him by the urgings of alarmed party rank and file? Or was it a calculated manoeuvre to replace the disappointing Austen Chamberlain and to return to public life?

Whatever their motives, Law and Baldwin saved the Conservative Party from the disunity which afflicted the Liberals, and thrust Lloyd George into the political wilderness from which he was never effectively to return.

A Prospects of a United Front Within the Coalition

You probably have not taken the trouble to see what has happened in the papers in regard to closer union. What happened was this – Lloyd George first of all met his Liberal Ministers and he found that they were much more frightened at the idea of losing their identity as Liberals and giving up the name than he had expected. In consequence when he met the Coalition Liberals as a whole he spoke only of the need for closer co-operation. The result of this is that any further step has in the meantime been postponed. What we are thinking of now is getting Resolutions passed by both sections approving of closer co-operation and suggesting that a Committee representative of both sides should be appointed to make proposals for this purpose. The result of this will probably be not to attempt any real fusion of the Parties but get co-operation something on the lines of the Liberal Unionists and Conservatives in the early days. This will be very difficult to arrange effectively and will certainly not be so efficient, but personally I am not sorry at the turn events have taken. I do not like the idea of complete fusion if it can be avoided but I had come to think, as I think you had also, that it was really inevitable if the Coalition were to continue, but it has always seemed to me more important from Lloyd George's point of view than from ours. As a Party we were losing nothing and since the necessity of going slowly in the matter has come from Lloyd George's own friends and not from ours I do not regret it.

From Bonar Law's letter to Balfour, 24 March 1920

B Austen Chamberlain Opposes a Dissolution, January 1922

Party grounds [for opposing a dissolution]:

(a) My object has been to lead the Unionist Party to accept merger in a new Party under the lead of the present Prime Minister and including the great bulk of the old Unionists and the old Liberals so as to secure the widest and closest possible union of all men and women of constitutional and progressive views. This requires time and careful preparation. No-one except myself has ever begun to touch it. An early dissolution would at best still find us a Coalition – which is both unsatisfactory and unpopular – and quite likely two independent and, not improbably, two hostile Parties. I am not sure that the mere talk of dissolution has not made my policy impossible.

(b) The feeling of my Party is almost universally against it.

(c) It would be a gamble in which the only things certain are that the Coalition would lose many seats and that many Unionists would refuse to stand as Coalitionists.

From Sir C. Petrie: *The Life and Letters of Austen Chamberlain*

C 'A Dynamic Force'

The Prime Minister was described this morning in *The Times*, in the words of a distinguished aristocrat, as a live wire. He was described to me, and to others, in more stately language, by the Lord Chancellor, as a dynamic force, and I accept those words. He is a dynamic force, and it is from that very fact that our troubles, in our opinion, arise. A dynamic force is a very terrible thing; it may crush but it is not necessarily right.

It is owing to that dynamic force, and that remarkable personality, that the Liberal Party, to which he formerly belonged, has been smashed to pieces; and it is my firm conviction that, in time, the same thing will happen to our party. We have already seen, during our association with him in the last four years, a section of our party hopelessly alienated. I think that if the present association is continued, and if this meeting agrees that it should be continued, you will see some more breaking up, and I believe the process must go on inevitably until the old Conservative party is smashed to atoms and lost in ruins.

I would like to give you just one illustration to show what I mean by the disintegrating influence of a dynamic force. Take Mr Chamberlain and myself . . . we are men who, I think, have exactly the same views on the political problems of the day . . . but the result of this dynamic force is that we stand here today, he prepared to go into the wilderness if he should be compelled to forsake the Prime Minister, and I prepared to go into the wilderness if I should be compelled to stay with him.

From Baldwin's speech at the Carlton Club, 19 October 1922

D A Comment on Baldwin's Part in the Downfall of the Coalition

Thereafter Baldwin was held up to the public gaze as a supreme example of patent honesty – the antithesis of the devious Lloyd George. It is strange that so few historians or biographers have pointed out the manifest contradiction. At the time when Baldwin made this speech he was still President of the Board of Trade and still a member of the Lloyd George Cabinet. He had never, so far as is known, raised any objection to the Government's policies or conveyed even the mildest protest to the Prime Minister himself. It is worth recording an entry in Lord Hankey's diary for the 21st October. He was attending a Guildhall luncheon:

'While we were awaiting the arrival of the Prince of Wales and I was standing among a group of Cabinet Ministers – Chamberlain, Worthington-Evans and others, Boscawen edged up to me and behaved in an offensively friendly manner. This annoyed me a good deal, because Boscawen, with Baldwin, was the 'Judas' of the Cabinet, who betrayed Chamberlain and Lloyd George at the Carlton Club, and his colleagues were distinctly giving him the cold shoulder at the Guildhall.'

The appellation is not undeserved. Baldwin may, as his biographers state, have been appalled at the 'moral disintegration' which had taken place under Lloyd George. Nevertheless he had continued to serve under his banmer without any protest whatsoever until it became expedient to overthrow him.

From Sir Dingle Foot: *British Political Crises* (1976)

Questions

1 Compare the views of Bonar Law (Source A) and Austen Chamberlain (Source B) concerning the merging of the Liberals and Conservatives in the Coalition into one party.   **(6 marks)**

2 'Baldwin's speech was effective not because of what he said, but because of the skill with which he said it.' How far does your study of Source C support this view?   **(7 marks)**

3 To what extent and for what reasons do you consider Sir Dingle Foot's account to be the work of an impartial historian?   **(7 marks)**

4 With reference both to these sources and to your own knowledge, explain why Baldwin and other Conservatives had become convinced that the Coalition should not continue.   **(10 marks)**

7 IRELAND

Parliament's refusal to accept Gladstone's solution to the Irish Question had profound political consequences. The Liberal Unionists were lost to the Liberal Party and soon strengthened and became indistinguishable from the Conservatives. For most of the 20 years from 1886–1905 the Conservatives were the party of government, and their preference for the label 'Unionists' until well into the 1920s was a public commitment to oppose Home Rule or worse, as well as a recognition of the renegade Liberals within their ranks. The Liberal Party throughout the 1890s was weakened by its commitment to Home Rule, and the role of the Lords in thwarting Home Rule was to be one important factor in preparing the way for the constitutional crisis of 1909–11. Meanwhile the Irish Nationalist Party was large enough and cohesive enough to hold the balance of power when the other parties, as in the years 1910–14, were evenly matched in numbers.

For Ireland, Gladstone's failure left a legacy of resentment and bitterness. The Conservative policy of killing Home Rule by kindness was mis-named, and ineffective in changing attitudes. Coercion and repression certainly brought a lessening of the violence from the 1890s onward, but it by no means disappeared. And although the subsidising and encouragement of land purchase and the extension to Ireland of local self-government largely removed Irish agrarian and political grievances, Irish commitment to Home Rule was an end in itself, and no longer (as it arguably was for many Irishmen in the 1870s and 1880s) a means to remedy religious, political and agrarian grievances.

Thus in 1910, when the Nationalists held the balance of power in Parliament, their price for supporting the Liberal attack on the House of Lords was Home Rule. Unable politically to prevent it, the Unionists on both sides of the Irish Sea resorted to opposition of dubious legality. The position of Conservative leaders such as Sir Edward Carson is often said to have bordered on treason. Certainly their inability to prevent Home Rule by constitutional methods made them do and say things which in calmer and more reflective moments they might regret. It is interesting to note that, less than a year after Unionist politicians seemed likely leaders in a civil war, they joined amicably with their Liberal opponents in a wartime coalition government. Nevertheless the situation seemed menacing enough at the beginning of 1914, and the so-called 'Curragh Mutiny' (when British Army officers appeared to stipulate whom they would and whom they would not fight) merely served to inflame the situation. How close Ireland came to civil war in 1914 is a matter of argument, but Home Rule became law even though its actual implementation was postponed because of the war.

At first the war restored a certain measure of calm to Ireland. The Nationalist leader John Redmond pledged his full support for the war and Catholic volunteers outnumbered Protestant ones in the Irish army recruiting offices. However, to some Irishmen the war was their opportunity. Home Rule was not enough, they wanted independence. The Sinn Fein Easter Rising of 1916 fired the imagination of those who wanted a free and independent Ireland, although they expected little to come of it. But it was the speed with which the British military authorities made martyrs of 15 of the rebels which turned a fiasco into a propaganda triumph. Sinn Fein begun to win Irish by-elections against Nationalist candidates, and the ill-judged and hastily abandoned proposal to extend conscription to Ireland in 1918 merely strengthened Sinn Fein's hold. In the general election of 1918 Sinn Fein swept the board in all predominantly Catholic areas of Ireland and the Nationalist Party was virtually annihilated. The newly elected Irish MPs declared themselves the representatives of an independent state, constituted themselves an independent parliament, the Dail, and waited for the British government to do its worst. It was now impossible to put into effect the Home Rule Act of 1914; it fell too far short of complete independence for Sinn Fein, and it came far too close to it for the Protestant community in the North.

At first the Coalition government favoured delay. But when violence became endemic the government compounded repressive terror with incompetence, strengthening the resolve of its Irish opponents and disgusting and shaming its Irish supporters. As some form of Home Rule or independence now seemed inevitable, its opponents, unable to preserve the union, turned to partition. A reluctant Conservative Party followed the Coalition leader Lloyd George in his quest for a solution. He for his part was dependent on Conservative backing, so could not grant full independence even if he had wanted to. The first major move, the Government of Ireland Act 1920, in fact set up a separate Northern Ireland parliament, and thus allayed some of the Conservative fears. Whether this was an unexpected or an anticipated result of the Act is a matter for controversy. However, now that Northern Ireland was a separate entity it was easier for the Unionists to go along with Home Rule, but this slowness to accept it and the extreme Nationalists' demand for independence and a republic led to further months of chaos and bloodshed against a background of political manoeuvrings.

Lloyd George's part in bringing about the Treaty of 1922 has aroused much controversy. Whether he deliberately deceived the Irish negotiators by promising a boundary Commission which would make Ulster unviable, and whether he combined this with a threat of force which was little more than a bluff, depends on conflicting and inadequate evidence. But Lloyd George had brought about Irish partition, secured an Irish settlement in which the Irish negotiators abandoned their more extreme positions, and led the Conservative Party to agree to virtual independence for southern Ireland. It was not a permanent solution, and it resulted in civil war in the south, but from 1923 it worked well enough, or at least peacefully enough, for several decades.

A Debate on the First Reading of the Home Rule Bill

The concluding day of the Home Rule debate, yesterday, provided a brilliant display of first-class Parliamentary oratory from the Irish benches. It provided also an object lesson to English observers of how little real danger there is in leaving the two sections of the Irish people to solve their troubles among themselves in their own way. There is no anger, no racial or religious bitterness that need be considered. The banter and chaff of Mr T.P. O'Connor, the profoundly clever sarcasm of Mr 'Tim' Healey [Irish Nationalist MPs], floated across the gangway to the Tory benches with the sparkle of a fresh rippling brook. There was nothing of the lashing fury of the storm wave . . .

Mr Walter Long [Conservative front bench spokesman], the ideal representative of that type of genuine British mediocrity which takes itself seriously, and the world around it even more seriously, resumed the discussion in a speech of many words. He had got all the old phrases off by heart, and he peeled them forth with an honest belief that they still have a telling effect.

He talked of the enemies of the British Government, of 'the men who have poured contempt upon and flouted everything which represents the British Empire', and he accused the Government of 'alienating, trampling upon, and insulting' the 'loyalists' of Ulster. He declared that the land legislation would 'strike a blow at the future prosperity of Ireland'. He denounced the Bill as 'stupid and unworkable', and speaking as an Irishman by adoption . . . he asserted on behalf of the 'loyalists' that no soft words delivered at the last moment would cajole them, no threats would disturb them. They believed in the path which lay before them. They would be true to the end whenever it might come.

It all sounded very terrible, delivered in a loud voice, with many gesticulations, by this rosy-faced, comfortable, and good-natured English squire, but it was a relic of bygone days and worn-out feuds.

From the *Northern Echo*, 17 April 1912

B 'Ulster 1912'

We know the war prepared
On every peaceful home,
We know the hells declared
For such as serve not Rome –

The terror, threats and dread
In market, hearth, and field –
We know, when all is said,
We perish if we yield.
What answer from the North?
One Law, one Land, one Throne.
If England drives us forth
We shall not fall alone.

From the poem by Rudyard Kipling

C Attitude of the Conservative Leader to the Irish Question

In our opposition to them [the Liberal ministers] we shall not be guided
by the consideration or bound by the restraints which would influence
us in an ordinary constitutional struggle. We shall take the means,
whatever means seem to us most effective, to deprive them of the
despotic power which they have usurped and compel them to appeal to
the people they have deceived. They may, perhaps they will, carry their
Home Rule Bill through the House of Commons but what then? I said
the other day in the House of Commons and I repeat here that there are
things stronger than parliamentary majorities.

Before I occupied the position which I now fill in the Party I said that,
in my belief, if an attempt were made to deprive these men of their
birthright – as part of a corrupt parliamentary bargain – they would be
justified in resisting such an attempt by all means in their power
including force. I said it then, and I repeat it now with a full sense of the
responsibility which attaches to my position, that if such an attempt is
made, I can imagine no length of resistance to which Ulster can go in
which I should not be prepared to support them, and in which, in my
belief, they would not be supported by the overwhelming majority of
the British people.

From a speech by Bonar Law to a Conservative meeting, 29 July 1912

D Ulster's Defiance

Being convinced in our consciences that Home Rule would be
disastrous to the material well-being of Ulster as well as of the whole of
Ireland, subversive of our civil and religious freedom, destructive of our
citizenship and perilous to the unity of the Empire, we, whose names
are underwritten, men of Ulster, loyal subjects of His Gracious Majesty
King George V, humbly relying on the God whom our fathers in days of
stress and trial confidently trusted, do hereby pledge ourselves in
solemn Covenant throughout this our time of threatened calamity to
stand by one another in defending for ourselves and our children our
cherished position of equal citizenship in the United Kingdom and in
using all means which may be found necessary to defeat the present

conspiracy to set up a Home Rule Parliament in Ireland. And in the event of such a Parliament being forced upon us we further solemnly and mutually pledge ourselves to refuse to recognise its authority.

In sure confidence that God will defend the right we hereto subscribe our names. . . .

Ulster's Solemn League and Covenant, 28 September 1912

E The Prime Minister's Account of the Curragh Incident

. . . I found here Winston Churchill. . . Sir John French and General Ewart – with some pretty alarming news. The Brigadier and about 57 officers of the Cavalry Brigade at the Curragh had sent in their resignations sooner than be employed in 'coercing' Ulster. The Brigadier – Gough – is a distinguished Cavalry officer, an Irishman, and the hottest of Ulsterians, and there can be little doubt that he has been using his influence with his subordinates to make them combine for a strike. We sent orders for him and the three colonels to come here at once and they will arrive this evening. Meanwhile, from what one hears today it seems likely that there was a misunderstanding. They seemed to have thought, from what Paget said, that they were about to be ordered off at once to shed the blood of the Covenanters, and they say they never meant to object to do duty like the other troops in protecting depots etc. and keeping order. This will be cleared up in a few hours, but there have been all sorts of agitations and alarums in high quarters, and I had a visit from Stamfordham [George V's secretary] who wore a very long face. I took the opportunity of saying that the main responsibility for all this mutinous [activity] rested with Lord Roberts, who is in a dangerous condition of senile frenzy.

From a letter written by Asquith, 21 March 1914

Questions

1 How effectively does the *Northern Echo* show its sympathies in Source A?
(**6 marks**)

2 From your own knowledge, do you consider the optimism of the *Northern Echo's* first paragraph to have been politically motivated, or do you consider that it had other contemporary justification? (**6 marks**)

3 How far does Kipling's poem (Source B) help to explain the attitude and fears of the Covenanters in Source D? (**6 marks**)

4 Bonar Law and other Conservative leaders have been accused of inciting rebellion in their speeches and in their support for the Covenant. Is this accusation borne out by Sources C and D? (**7 marks**)

5 From your own knowledge:
   a) Explain the reference to 'a corrupt parliamentary bargain' in Source C. **(5 marks)**
   b) Explain the importance of the references to George V in Sources D and E. **(6 marks)**

6 'Asquith was weak and indecisive'. Does Source E show him in this light? **(4 marks)**

7 Using these sources and your own knowledge, comment on the view that in the circumstances of 1912–14 no solution to the Irish Problem was likely to be found. **(10 marks)**

8 THE RISE OF THE

LABOUR PARTY 1900–24

The formation of the Independent Labour Party in 1893 and the creation of the Labour Representation Committee in 1900 did not bring about a united left-wing voice in Parliament. Although the LRC was successful in securing 29 seats in 1906, there were still 14 miners' MPs who held aloof from their LRC colleagues at least on some important issues, and there were still about a dozen MPs who could be called Lib-Lab. The neo-Marxist Social Democratic Federation had refused to join the LRC in 1900 and 1911 it was so discontented with the moderation of the LRC's policies that it joined with others to form the British Socialist Party, which was to enjoy no parliamentary success.

Working-class poverty and working-class discontent with the old parties, combined with a growing sense of economic power arising from successful strikes such as the Dock Strike of 1889, help to explain the growing popularity of Labour. But it would be a mistake to underestimate here the efforts of the LRC to avoid being identified with class, and it did have the support of middle-class intellectuals who felt that only through an acceptable left-wing party could necessary changes in society be brought about.

In the years before 1914 the main concerns of Labour MPs were to reverse the hostile Taff Vale and Osborne judgments. This committed them to supporting the Liberal government, particularly during the crisis of 1909–11. It has been alleged that the Liberals, while quick to reverse Taff Vale in 1906, deliberately delayed reversing the Osborne judgment by a new Trade Disputes Act until 1913 in order to tie the Labour members to keeping the Liberal government in power at least until the Lords and Irish questions were safely dealt with. But there is no doubt that the reversal of the judgments and the introduction of payment of MPs in 1911 paved the way for greater Labour representation in Parliament.

The First World War brought mixed results for Labour. At first the reluctance of some of its leaders to go to war was confused with pacificism and undermined the party's popularity. Ramsay MacDonald even found it necessary to resign as secretary. But Asquith's coalition government in 1915 included Labour's Arthur Henderson, and three Labour members joined Lloyd George's new ministry in December 1916. Internal wrangling over such issues as conscription and a compromise peace prevented the Labour Party from taking full advantage of the Liberal split; it even gave Lloyd Geoge the opportunity to humiliate Henderson and to force his resignation from the Cabinet. However, as this gave Henderson the time and incentive to help Labour draw up its war aims and to agree on a peace time policy of evolutionary socialism, Lloyd George had done himself a disservice. Henderson would not now or in the future seriously consider collaboration with Lloyd George. The newly reorganised Labour Party determined to fight the 1918 general election as an independent party with a progressive policy. While Lloyd George, the radical, was now leader of a predominantly Conservative government, the Labour Party's 63 seats made it the largest of the opposition parties (the Asquith Liberals secured only 30). To the electorate, Labour began to appear as the natural alternative to the Conservatives.

Weaknesses in the leadership and lack of intellectual vigour among some of its MPs did not seem to handicap Labour. It more than doubled its parliamentary representation in 1922, and increased it again in 1923 despite the large negative vote for the Liberals who had temporarily reunited against tariff reform. Labour had disappointed those who had confidently predicted that as a revolutionary party it could not be a responsible opposition. And although MacDonald had pronounced against Labour ever forming a minority government necessitating a partnership with another party, he abandoned that position in his determination to show that Labour could be responsible in government, too.

Thus Labour formed its first minority government in January 1924 dependent on Liberal support. It is arguable how successful it was. In domestic affairs the Liberals prevented it from carrying out the far-reaching reforms of its policy commitment, but some improvements in social benefits were achieved and the Wheatley Housing Act was still successfully operating in the 1930s. In foreign affairs there were some significant achievements, among them the Geneva Protocol and reconciliation with Russia. However, the government could hardly expect to enjoy Liberal co-operation indefinitely. The manner in which the Liberals brought the government down over the Campbell affair is of interest, if only because some historians have seen in it Baldwin's dexterity in saddling the Liberals with the electoral liability of having prematurely ended the Labour experiment. Government incompetence in handling the Zinoviev Letter is a matter of greater import than whether Baldwin knew the letter was a fake (he probably did not), or whether Conservative Central Office knew it was (it probably did). But at least Labour had enjoyed power without abusing it; it had accepted the restraints of Britain's type of parliamentary democracy and proved that it was fit to be entrusted with government again. In that sense, as well as in years, the parliamentary Labour Party by 1924 had come of age.

A Co-operation Between the Liberal Party and Labour

1. No compact alliance agreement or bargain.
2. There being no material points of difference in the main lines of

Liberal policy we are ready to ascertain from qualified and responsible
Labour leaders how far Labour candidates can be given an open field
against a common enemy.

3. We are ready to do this as an act of friendship and without any
stipulation of any kind, because we realise that an accession of strength
to Labour representation in the House of Commons is not only required
by the country in the interests of Labour but that it would increase
progressive forces generally and the Liberal Party as the best available
instrument of progress.

The question then arises how and where can this open field be
secured?

4. The Liberal Council is bound to act for and with recognised local
Liberal Associations and this principle cannot be departed from *under
any circumstances*. On the other hand, the Liberal Council can use its
influence with the local associations to abstain from nominating a
Liberal candidate, and to unite in support of any recognised and
competent Labour candidate who supports the general objects of the
Liberal Party . . .

9. It must, however, be distinctly understood that if in any agreed
constituency the Liberal local association breaks away and runs a
Liberal candidate, the Liberal Council must support that candidate.

From a memorandum by the Liberal Chief Whip on his electoral agreement
with the Secretary of the Labour Representation Committee, 13 March 1903

B Common Ground Between Liberal and Labour Policies

They had heard it said that it was impossible for Liberalism and Labour
to work together. He had been twenty years in the Commons, and had
taken a fair share in the work of the House with regard to land and
Labour. On every issue he could remember, where the rights of Labour
were concerned, he had found Liberals and Labour men fighting side by
side. Where was the real difference of view between Socialists and
thorough-going Liberals like himself? If it was Socialism for a State to
insist that adult men should have reasonable hours of Labour, then they
were all Socialists . . .

Take 'Graduated taxation'. Where was the difference on that? Liberals
wanted a graduated Income Tax to relieve the poor man, absolutely fair
taxation as between one man and another. The Liberals, must as
Socialists, wanted taxation of land values. If Socialism meant that they
should check physical deterioration by getting children fed properly
before school, then they were all Socialists . . .

John Burns was one of his best friends. On his 'Old Age Pensions Bill'
– introduced again that year – to prove that question was a living issue –
he had the name of Mr Keir Hardie. On all the three other occasions the
Trades Disputes Bill was balloted for by many Liberals, and on those

three other occasions the Bill was brought in by prominent Liberal Imperialists . . . So they had on the side of Labour not only men like himself, but strong representatives of the Imperialist wing also . . .

He cared not whether a man called himself Socialist, or Independent Labour, or Social Democrat, or any other name under heaven. If he was working for the benefit of his fellow men, he was with him, and with him with all his heart.

From a report of a speech by the Liberal MP Sir Francis Channing, 13 September 1905

C The 'Red Scare'

It is indispensable to stir up the masses of the British proletariat, to bring into movement the army of unemployed proletarians. It is imperative that the group in the Labour Party sympathising with the treaty (between Britain and Russia) should bring increased pressure to bear upon the government and parliamentary circles in favour of ratification of the treaty . . .

A settlement of relations between the two countries [Britain and Russia] will assist in the revolutionising of the international and British proletariat not less than a successful rising in any of the working districts of England, as the establishment of close contact between the British and Russian proletariat, the exchange of delegations and workers, etc., will make it possible for us to extend and develop the propaganda of ideas of Leninism in England and the Colonies. Armed warfare must be preceded by a struggle against the inclinations to compromise which are embedded among the majority of British workmen, against the ideas of evolution and the peaceful extermination of capitalism. Only then will it be possible to count upon complete success of an armed insurrection . . . agitation-propaganda work in the army is weak, in the navy a very little better . . . [There should be cells] in all units of the troops particularly among those quartered in large centres . . . and also among factories working on munitions and at military store depots . . . In the event of danger of war, with the aid of the latter and in contact with the transport workers, it is possible to paralyse all the military preparations of the bourgeoisie and make a start in turning an imperialist war into a class war.

From the Zinoviev Letter, October 1924

D Punch's View of the Liberal-Labour Relationship

FORCED FELLOWSHIP.

SUSPICIOUS-LOOKING PARTY. "ANY OBJECTION TO MY COMPANY, GUV'NOR? I'M AGOIN' YOUR WAY"—(aside) "AND FURTHER."

Punch cartoon, 27 October 1909

E A Cartoonist revives memories of the Zinoviev Letter

"DEAR, DEAR! SURELY Mr. ZINOVIEV HASN'T MISSED THE POST!"

Cartoon by Low in the *Evening Standard*, May 1929

Questions

1 Do you agree that from the evidence of Source A the electoral agreement appears to be of greater advantage to the Liberals than to Labour? **(5 marks)**

2 Using Source B and your own knowledge, show how far and why Channing highlights the similarities but ignores the differences between Liberals and Labour in 1905. **(6 marks)**

3 How different are the views of Channing as expressed in Source B and the cartoonist as expressed in Source D? **(6 marks)**

4 'Anyone with a knowledge of or sympathy with Communism could have written the Zinoviev Letter.' Does your study of the text of Source C support this view? **(6 marks)**

5 From your own knowledge and from the source, explain the message and purpose of the cartoonist in Source E. **(6 marks)**

6 Is is reasonable, from these sources and from your own knowledge, to support the view that the more powerful the Labour Party became the more desperate its opponents were to discredit it? **(7 marks)**

9 THE GENERAL STRIKE
1926

Historians in their search for the origins of the General Strike have often given an impression of its inevitability which would have surprised its leaders. The Labour defeat in 1924, the union oscillation between political and industrial action, the determination of extremists on both sides for a showdown, the parlous state of the mining industry, the creation of the General Council of the Trade Union Congress in 1920 – all seemed to make a union challenge to the government likely. The disaster of 'Black Friday', 1921, in which collaboration between the major unions in an industrial dispute collapsed, made the TUC determined not to suffer such humiliation again.

Yet it is just as plausible to argue that the General Strike was not planned, that it took both unions and government by surprise, and that it came about by accident. The threat of limited TUC support for the miners in July 1925 led the government to grant a nine-month subsidy and a Royal Commission. Some historians (e.g. Cole and Postgate in *The Common People*) have accused the government of deliberately buying time in order to smash the unions. The government did, indeed, make contingency plans for a general strike – after 'Black Friday' earlier governments had acted similarly – but it was its duty to take precautions against this possibility, however unlikely. Baldwin hoped that the Samuel Commission's recommendations would be sufficiently attractive to enable the miners to make some concessions to the mine owners and thus bring about a satisfactory solution. It is unlikely that, at a time of falling prices, his acceptance of the need for *some* reduction in miners' wages was part of a planned confrontation. What no-one had really anticipated was the absolute intransigence of the mine owners; perhaps they hoped for a renewed subsidy, or perhaps theirs was simply an automatic response – even members of the Conservative government regarded them as stupid. In the event, the 'lock-out' of the miners brought a very reluctant TUC to threaten a general strike. It also brought the TUC and the government together in an effort to avoid one. If Churchill and Birkenhead were hot-heads spoiling for a fight, there was no such behaviour on the TUC side. Agreement was close but foundered over the miners' reluctance to agree, and the government's belief that the issue of strike notices and the isolated action of the printers' union made a settlement impossible. Thus the TUC was plunged into a general strike which it did not want, and for which it was not prepared, and the government found it necessary to implement its contingency plans.

The General Strike was conducted with much good humour and

restraint, but there was some sporadic violence and disorder. As the strike was an attempt by the TUC to put pressure on the government, Baldwin was able to represent it as a challenge to the constitution. Here he was attacking the TUC's weakness because it drew back from any kind of illegal action and wanted the strike to be no more than an extension of an ordinary industrial dispute. The government control of the media gave it an edge in the propaganda war, and its Organisation for the Maintenance of Supplies limited public inconvenience mainly to transport difficulties.

It may be that some of the TUC leaders were looking for an excuse to abandon the strike, not because it was ineffective, but because they were frightened of where control of such a powerful weapon was leading them. Moreover, throughout the strike the miners had held aloof from the TUC management and control of it: so the TUC was not really aware of how much the miners were prepared to concede in search of a compromise solution – it suspected very little. Thus Sir Herbert Samuel's intervention, in which, on his initiative, he suggested that an agreement should be based on his own report of March 1926 with some minimal changes in favour of the miners, was welcomed by the TUC which was having increasing doubts about the legality of the strike. As the government had not authorised Samuel's offer the TUC abandonment of the strike was, in effect, unconditional surrender, although Baldwin was probably sincere in his promises which were intended to help the TUC save face.

The TUC's abandonment of the miners caused much bitterness, and a prolonged miners' strike ended with humiliation for the miners. Baldwin's promises could not prevent victimisation for other strikers, and he did not effectively resist the 1926 Tory Party Conference's demand for revenge, nor that of some of his Cabinet, so that the Trades Disputes Act of 1927 followed. Perhaps Baldwin's influence prevented it from being more savage, but he had opposed similar legislation in 1925. Much has been made of the decline in trade union membership after the General Strike. Probably only a few on the extremist fringes actually abandoned membership, but recruitment slowed down, and rising unemployment would take its own toll of membership. Perhaps the General Strike had some residual effect on the general election result in 1929, but there were other reasons for the Conservative defeat, and despite the inferiority in parliamentary seats the Conservatives polled more votes than Labour. It was probably the experience of the General Strike itself rather than the subsequent Trade Disputes Act which tied the TUC more firmly to the Labour Party, and weighted it more heavily towards political rather than industrial pursuit of its objectives.

A The Case for the TUC

The General Council of the Trade Union Congress last night issued the following message:

The trade unions are fighting in defence of the mine-workers. The responsibility for the national crisis lies with the Government.

With the people the trade unions have no quarrel. On the contrary, the unions are fighting to maintain the standard of life of the great mass of the people.

The trade unions have not entered upon this struggle without counting the cost. They are assured that the trade unionists of the country, realising the justice of the cause they are called upon to support, will stand loyally by their elected leaders until the victory and an honourable peace has been won.

The need now is for loyalty, steadfastness and unity.

The General Council of the Trade Union Congress appeals to the workers to follow the instructions that have been issued by their union leaders.

Let none be disturbed by rumours or be driven by panic to betray the cause.

Violence and disorder must everywhere be avoided no matter what the incitement.

Stand firm and we shall win.

From a report in the *Daily Herald,* 4 May 1926

B The Case for the Government

MESSAGE FROM THE PRIME MINISTER

Constitutional government is being attacked

Let all good citizens whose livelihood and labour have thus been put in peril bear with fortitude and patience the hardships with which they have been so suddenly confronted.

Stand behind the government who are doing their part confident that you will co-operate in the measures they have undertaken to preserve the liberties and privileges of the people of these islands.

The laws of England are the peoples' birthright.

The laws are in your keeping.

You have made Parliament their guardian.

The General Strike is a challenge to Parliament and is the road to anarchy and ruin.

STANLEY BALDWIN

The strike is intended as a direct hold-up of the nation to ransom . . . 'This moment,' as the Prime Minister pointed out in the House of Commons, 'has been chosen to challenge the existing Constitution of the country and to substitute the reign of force for that which now exists . . . I do not believe there has been anything like a thorough-going consultation with the rank and file before this despotic power was put in the hands of a small executive in London . . . I do not think all the leaders who assented to order a general strike fully realised that they were threatening the basis of ordered government and coming nearer to proclaiming civil war than we have been for centuries past.'

From the *British Gazette*, 6 May 1926

C The TUC's Reply

The General Council does not challenge the Constitution. It is not seeking to substitute unconstitutional government. Nor is it desirous of undermining our Parliamentary institutions. The sole aim of the Council is to secure for the miners a decent standard of life. The Council is engaged in an industrial dispute. There is no constitutional crisis . . .

It is fantastic for the Prime Minister to pretend that the trade unions are engaged in an attack upon the Constitution of the country. Every instruction issued by the General Council is evidence of their determination to maintain the struggle strictly on the basis of an industrial dispute. They have ordered every member taking part to be exemplary in his conduct and not to give any cause for police interference. The General Council struggled hard for peace. They are anxious that an honourable peace shall be secured as soon as possible. They are not attacking the Constitution. They are not fighting the community. They are defending the mine-workers against the mine-owners.

From the *British Worker*, 7 May 1926

D The View Taken by Punch

THE LEVER BREAKS.

From *Punch*, May 1926

E The Legality of the General Strike

The central proposition which I suggest that anyone who studies this matter fairly must accept, is this – that this so-called 'general strike', whatever be the provocation or explanation or the circumstances which caused it to be decided on, is not, properly understood, a trade dispute at all. A strike is a strike against employers to compel employers to do something, but a General Strike is a strike against the general public to make the public, Parliament and the Government do something.

From a speech in the House of Commons by Sir John Simon, 11 May 1926

Questions

1 How far does Source A support or contradict the view that the TUC was not wholly committed to the General Strike? **(4 marks)**

2 Comment on the effectiveness of Source B as a piece of propaganda. **(5 marks)**

3 From your own knowledge consider whether Source C gives an accurate representation of how the TUC conducted the General Strike. **(5 marks)**

4 'As Source D is biased it is of little value to an historian.' Do you agree? **(4 marks)**

5 Source E is Sir John Simon's elaboration on his view that the General Strike was illegal, but his argument has been described as simplistic. Do you agree? **(4 marks)**

6 From your own knowledge and from the sources comment on the opinion that the General Strike was 'more a war of words than a war of deeds.' **(8 marks)**

10 BALDWIN

Baldwin has always been something of an enigma both to his contemporaries and to historians. Stanley Baldwin liked to present himself as honest and simple, a man of honour who was not necessarily always right, but who always believed that what he was doing was for the public good; he did not seek greatness, but had it thrust upon him by contemporary circumstances. To his critics, however, he was devious, schemed for high office, ruined Lloyd George's career, outwitted and outmanoeuvred MacDonald, lied to his electorate on rearmament, and owed his advancement to luck rather than to talent.

Both views need modification. Baldwin began his political career later than some of his contemporaries (i.e. Churchill) and by 1914, after six years in Parliament, had done little to distinguish himself. Through a friend's recommendation he was given office in Asquith's wartime Coalition government and he remained in office under Lloyd George. If he had an obsession it was for the strengthening of the Conservative Party, and his break with Lloyd George in 1922 was to preserve party unity; he fully expected his own career to end with failure, not success, at the Carlton Club meeting. Instead he was fortunate that the leading Conservatives at first remained loyal to Lloyd George so that Bonar Law had to promote him in 1922. Then, in 1923, with Balfour, Chamberlain and Curzon all for various reasons out of the running, he found himself, to his own surprise and that of the country, as prime minister. His suicidal adoption of tariff reform in 1923 can be seen as an attempt to force Lloyd George to tie himself to free trade, and to make the centre party Lloyd George was hankering for impossible. In this way the Conservative Party was preserved intact, despite its electoral defeat.

Baldwin's patent honesty and sincerity meant that he cultivated friendships across the political divides. His opponents believed that he genuinely desired a compromise settlement in 1926, and when the General Strike ended he refrained, although his party did not, from gloating over the TUC's unconditional surrender. One critic, while asserting that Baldwin hated decisions and preferred procrastination and compromise, claimed that he was better at dealing with other politicians than Lloyd George, because Baldwin had observed them closely as men, while Lloyd George simply saw them as inanimate pieces on a chess board. So Baldwin was willing to give Labour the chance to prove itself as a parliamentary rather than a revolutionary party, both in 1923 and in 1929; and in 1931 Baldwin was willing to work with MacDonald. While some accused him of doing anything to achieve and retain power, others accused him of laziness and a lack of ambition, and a willingness to let MacDonald take the responsibility for necessary unpopular measures. It may be that both criticisms are wide of the mark. Baldwin had no great understanding of international economics, and he may have thought the National Government essential for national survival. Some cynics see 1931 as a Baldwin plot to discredit and split Labour and to entrench the Conservatives in power, but such deviousness would have been difficult to achieve in the face of the sudden and unexpected crisis, and given Baldwin's slowness to make decisions.

It seems doubtful that if Baldwin had been obsessed with power he would have been content to accept MacDonald's leadership for four years. Yet, despite the fact that MacDonald was, after the 1931 general election, in thrall to the Conservative Party, Baldwin accepted second place, and there is no evidence of any intrigue to remove MacDonald. Baldwin replaced him in due course in 1935, got into increasing difficulties in foreign affairs, not least because of his 'appalling frankness' to the electorate, but was saved by the Abdication Crisis. This he handled with consummate skill and decision, and Baldwin's contemporaries credited him with saving the monarchy and the Empire. He thus was able to retire in 1937 with a largely untarnished reputation.

But by 1939 and 1940 all had changed. Baldwin was reviled by those who saw him as an architect of appeasement, even by those politicians who had consistently voted against his efforts to increase defence spending. Thus his ultimate reputation is bound up with the verdict on appeasement, but no-one can deny him his political pre-eminence during the 1920s and 1930s, even if historians continue to argue over his abilities and achievements.

A Baldwin's Style

(i) I am a man of peace. I am longing, and working, and praying for peace. But I will not surrender the safety and security of the British constitution. You placed me in power 18 months ago by the largest majority accorded to any party for many, many years. Have I done anything to forfeit that confidence? Cannot you trust me to ensure a square deal to secure even justice between man and man?

From Baldwin's radio broadcast during the General Strike, 9 May 1926

(ii) The personal note does not come easily to an Englishman, but I am speaking to you, my fellow countrymen, mostly in the quietness of your own homes in every corner of the land, and may I put it to you in this way in half-a-dozen words? – You trusted me before, I ask you to trust me again.

From Baldwin's general election broadcast, 29 May 1929

(iii) I put before the whole House my own views with an appalling frankness. From 1933 I and my friends were all very worried about what was happening in Europe . . . I am speaking of 1933 and 1934. You will remember the election at Fulham in the autumn of 1933, when a seat which the National Government held was lost by about 7,000 votes on no issue but the pacifist. You will remember perhaps about the National Government candidate who made a most guarded reference to the question of defence and was mobbed for it.

That was the feeling of the country in 1933. My position as a leader of a great party was not altogether a comfortable one. I asked myself what chance was there – when that feeling that was given expression to in Fulham was common throughout the country – what chance was there within the next year or two of that feeling being so changed that the country would give a mandate for rearmament? . . .

I think the country itself learned by certain events that took place during the winter of 1934–5 what the perils might be to it . . . [So in 1935] we got from the country – with a large majority – a mandate for doing a thing that no-one, 12 months before, would have believed possible.

From Baldwin's speech in the House of Commons, 12 November 1936

B A Newspaper's Criticism of Baldwin

The new and the great authority on the democratic system is Earl Baldwin . . . It was on November 12, 1936 that Lord Baldwin, then plain Mister, arose in the House of Commons. He said he had not told the electors the truth about rearmament at the 1935 general election because he believed that if he had done so they would not have voted for him. Lord Baldwin did more damage to democracy than any other Premier in Britain, and certainly more damage than any other man except Cromwell. For eight years, as long as he was Premier of Great Britain, he drew his breath, his pipe and his salary. Except for the fact that he has now exchanged his salary for an ex-Premier's pension of £2,000 a year, he is drawing all three still.

From the *Sunday Express*, 3 September 1939

C An Historian's Comment on Baldwin's First Premiership

The new Prime Minister was the Conservative leader, Bonar Law, whose almost immediate retirement, on the point of death, resulted in a scramble for the leadership.

The choice fell on Baldwin who was a loyal party man and who, unlike Austen Chamberlain and Lord Curzon, had not made personal enemies. He was also very different from Lloyd George, unlikely to get involved in crises like that at Chanak, a man who might be expected to usher in a quiet time. He was quickly able to create his own legend as 'Honest

Stan'; with the coming of radio, indeed, he was able to present himself as the nation's uncle, calmly unfolding his policies to the people through their wirelesses and inspiring every confidence. In a man of such virtue, ability seemed to be of secondary importance.

From J.B. Watson: *Success in Twentieth Century World Affairs* (1974)

D An Historian's Assessment of Baldwin

[Baldwin's] power and ability came from his apparent lack of them; people trusted him, and they did trust him – because he appeared to be *not* a politician, but the plain man in politics. And in part this was true: his policy was to have no policy; he never had a plan ahead of a gathering crisis; he hated coming to decisions, and to do so made him physically nervous, so that his hands would twitch. He was, in fact, a very sensitive person, behind his bovine mask. When in doubt, he preferred to do nothing, hoping that things would settle themselves. He admitted that he was a lazy man. He liked nothing better than to sit in his inner room, playing patience or doing a crossword puzzle or reading a novel or a biography. In a crisis he would withdraw to his sanctum; or if it was acute, go to bed.

From C.L. Mowat: *Britain Between the Wars* (1955)

E Baldwin and MacDonald Compared

MacDonald had already suffered the obloquy of a man who was alleged to have betrayed his party, but there lay ahead of Baldwin the years till his death in 1947 during which he was despised as the man who had allegedly betrayed his country by failing to arm it for war against Hitler's Germany. The contempt in which he was held in the decade after 1937 was itself somewhat contemptible, but there can be no denying that neither he nor MacDonald had much to contribute to the nation once the 1920s had collapsed into the chaos of the 1930s. Soporifics and sedatives had their value during the acute domestic tensions of the 1920s, but the 1930s called for different qualities. Baldwin and MacDonald were deficient in intellectual power, sluggish in temperament and possessed of a squalid dislike of men of drive and personality. Baldwin, in particular, peopled his governments with men so mediocre that, among them, Neville Chamberlain could rightly be looked upon as his successor by undisputed title. This was perhaps Baldwin's real disservice to his country.

From L.C.B. Seaman: *Post-Victorian Britain, 1902–1951* (first pub. 1966)

Questions

1 What are the uses and limitations to an historian of the three extracts in Source A? **(6 marks)**

2 Using the two sources only, consider how justified is Source B in its criticism of the speech in Source A (iii). **(6 marks)**

3 Comparing Sources C, D and E, explain which you regard as the most hostile in its criticism of Baldwin. **(8 marks)**

4 Using the sources and your own knowledge, write your own historical assessment of Baldwin. **(10 marks)**

11 LABOUR IN POWER
1929–31

The Labour government of 1929–31 is remembered mainly for the circumstances and manner of its downfall. It is regarded as a resumption of the minority government of 1923–4, and its achievements are often dismissed as largely irrelevant to the economic whirlwind that was about to engulf the industrial world.

In one sense the second Labour government was an advance on its predecessor; at least it had a greater claim to govern, as Labour was for the first time the largest single party in the House of Commons. But it could no more carry out socialist policies than it could in 1923–4; its continued existence depended on the tolerance of the Liberals, and the unlikelihood of Conservatives and Liberals combining to bring it down. Thus it could neither promote nationalisation nor repeal the Trades Disputes Act. Even so, with strong leadership and the courage of its convictions it might have pursued an economic policy designed to tackle unemployment and promote prosperity. Instead it regarded the Gold Standard as sacrosanct for fear of inflation, and balanced budgets as sacrosanct for fear of a run on the pound. Keynes's and Mosley's proposals for public spending to reduce unemployment were regarded as profligate. Thus road programmes which might have built *autobahns* and employed hundreds of thousands ended up as the temporary employment of a few thousand to remove some level crossings.

It was somewhat naive for some ex-ministers to complain, after the National Government came off the Gold Standard, that 'I did not know that we could have done that'. What Churchill had done in 1925 they could have undone at any time, but Snowden was too orthodox and MacDonald too timid, and the opportunity was never grasped.

The government did, however, achieve something worthwhile in slum clearance, and in proposing marketing boards in agriculture. Needless to say, these measures would not have been passed had they been specifically socialist, and the National Government was later to make good use of both of them. In other fields the government brought enthusiasm to the international disarmament talks, and began to grapple with the problem of India.

Because of Labour's minority position it was to be expected that MacDonald would negotiate with other parties for closer co-operation. In this he failed, but it would be reading too much into his tentative overtures to Lloyd George (whom he personally disliked) to suggest, as some historians have done, that MacDonald was working for a national government as soon as he entered office. That was to come from a national economic crisis, and not from the devious schemes of a man allegedly plotting for two years to betray his party.

A MacDonald Asks for Co-operation from the Other Parties

I want to say something else. It is not because I happen to be at the head of a minority that I say this. The thought must be occurring to the minds of everyone who is aware of the very serious problems that this country has to face . . . I wonder how far it is possible, without in any way abandoning any of our party positions, without in any way surrendering any item of our party principles, to consider ourselves more as a Council of State, and less as arrayed regiments facing each other in battle . . . So far as we are concerned, co-operation will be welcomed . . . so that by putting our ideas into a common pool we can bring out legislation and administration that will be of substantial benefit for the nation as a whole.

From MacDonald's speech in the House of Commons, 2 July 1929

B Lloyd George's Defence of the Liberal Policy of Keeping the Second Labour Government in Power

There are some who say look neither to the right nor to the left but keep straight on. (A delegate: 'Hear, hear . . .')

Ah, my friend, before the war there was a great ship set out on its maiden voyage across the Atlantic. A message came over the ether 'there are icebergs on the course you are pursuing'. But the captain looked neither to the right nor to the left; he went straight on. Let me say here and now I am opposed to *Titanic* seamanship in politics and as an old mariner I would not drive the ship onto the icy floes that have drifted into our seas from the frozen wastes of the Tory past. If the National Liberal Federation in its wisdom this afternoon decides to take another course I would advise my friends to put on their life-belts and plant their deckchairs as near as possible to the boats; unless, of course, any of them have already made arrangements to be picked up.

From Lloyd George's speech to the Liberal Conference, May 1931

C Prospects for Closer Co-operation

Generally speaking Labour would like an alliance. They would be willing to drop certain of their present ministers . . . Ramsay would be Prime Minister. Lloyd George would be at the Foreign Office or the Treasury. Ramsay thinks he can adjourn early in August and resume late in the autumn, and then continue till the next budget. No fear of immediate Election. It might be contemplated that the Army, Air and Navy join up under one ministry.

From a memorandum by Lloyd George, July 1931

D The Deficit in the Unemployment Fund

Under present conditions the income and expenditure of the Unemployment Fund balance when 900,000 persons are qualified for Insurance benefit. The decrease in contribution income is about £350,000 per annum for each 100,000 persons added to the Live Register while the increase in benefit paid is about £4,500,000. Assuming that the average Live Register is 2,500,000 . . . the beneficiaries are drawing out of the Unemployment Fund more than two and a half times the amount paid in contributions by employers and workers . . .

The following is a summary of the measures which we recommend to deal with the present situation pending our final Report . . .

In order that the income and expenditure of the Unemployment Fund may be brought more closely to balancing point with a Live Register of 2,500,000 we recommend:

1. A limit upon the period for which benefit may be paid of 26 weeks within the 12 months following the date of application.

2. An increase in the weekly rates of contributions so that, in the case of adult men, each of the three parties (the worker, the employer and the Exchequer) pays 9d. with appropriate increases in the rate of contributions for other classes.

3. An amendment [i.e. reduction] of the weekly rates of unemployment benefit . . .

From the first report of the Royal Commission on Unemployment Insurance, June 1931

E Numbers Claiming Unemployment Benefit

(numbers in millions)

1929	1.2
1930	1.9
1931	2.7

(adapted)

F The Approaching Crisis, An Historian's View

On the Government's right the financiers clamoured for the drastic retrenchment in public expenditure by cutting down the social services and especially by reducing benefits to the unemployed and depriving as many as possible of them of any sort of dole. They demanded that any domestic sacrifice necessary for the maintenance of the gold standard and the profit system should be made for the poor. Supported by Chancellor Snowden, a whole-hearted convert to 'sound finance', they badgered Ramsay MacDonald with their prophecies of disaster, until he came to believe with them that the one thing needful for economic salvation was that the Government should enjoy the fullest confidence of the capitalist class.

From G.D.H. Cole and R. Postgate: *The Common People, 1746–1948* (1938)

Questions

1 Was Ramsay MacDonald arguing for a coalition government in Source A? Explain your answer. **(5 marks)**

2 a) Is Source B an effective defence to the charge that the Liberals were keeping MacDonald in power? **(5 marks)**
b) What was Lloyd George hinting at (Source B) in suggesting that some Liberals may 'have already made arrangements to be picked up'? **(3 marks)**

3 Using only the evidence of Source D, explain the likely reasons why the Labour government chose to ignore the Report of the Royal Commission. **(5 marks)**

4 a) How does Source F reveal the prejudices of its authors? **(6 marks)**
b) Do any of the other sources give justification to the view put forward in Source F? Explain your answer. **(4 marks)**

5 Using sources D–F and your own knowledge, explain why the second Labour government found unemployment so difficult a problem to tackle. **(7 marks)**

12 THE CRISIS OF 1931

The financial crisis of August 1931 should not have taken the government by surprise. The Wall Street Crash had rocked the financial markets in 1929, and since then unemployment in Britain had been steadily rising while exports fell. When MacDonald first thought of a coalition to tackle the economic crisis is a matter of controversy, but certainly by the early summer of 1931 he would have preferred all-party support for any necessary measures. But the government was shackled in various ways: by its lack of a parliamentary majority, by its commitment to orthodox economics, and by its dependence on foreign loans. All-party support would hardly have given it greater freedom of action.

It was easy afterwards to say that there were alternative financial and economic policies that ought to have been pursued. Some (e.g. Mosley's) the government had already positively rejected, while others it did not believe were available. Even Keynes, subsequently the guru of economic thinking, shifted his ground during the crisis. No-one in the government had enough understanding of economics to challenge Snowden effectively; those who did mainly opposed his specific cuts, not his overall strategy. So whether it was a 'bankers' ramp' or not, the government certainly believed that it faced the herculean task of balancing the budget and preventing a run on the pound.

The notion of a MacDonald plot to bring about coalition and abandon socialism is difficult to take seriously. It may be that socialism to MacDonald was more a utopian dream than a programme of specific measures. Yet in the political circumstances of 1929–31 a socialist programme was out of the question. The immediate issue in August 1931 was whether MacDonald should admit failure and resign, or whether he should place country above party and lead a national crusade to tackle the crisis. In deciding on the latter he seems to have responded to the urgings of George V, rather than to personal ambition. He was certainly flattered by the pressure put on him to stay on as prime minister, but he was under no illusions. While he was later to resent the disloyalty of so many of his party, he advised junior ministers in the Labour government not to join or support the National Government in order to safeguard their future careers.

The general election result of 1931 put MacDonald in a position reminiscent of that of Lloyd George in 1918. Perhaps MacDonald was naive enough to think that he might be able to avoid splitting his party and preserve a strong Labour nucleus in the new Parliament. Yet his party had already rejected him before the election, and he described the election result, with its massive Conservative representation, as a disaster. MacDonald's services to the Labour Party were soon forgotten by his former supporters; they now regarded him as a traitor to his party rather than a hapless victim of circumstance.

A The Bank of England's Analysis of the Crisis

[It told the government] (1) that we were on the edge of the precipice and, unless the situation changed rapidly, we should be over it directly, (2) that the cause of the trouble was not financial but political, and lay in complete want of confidence in His Majesty's Government existing among foreigners, (3) that the remedy was in the hands of the Government alone.

The Bank of England's message to MacDonald and Snowden, 11 August 1931

B Baldwin's Subsequent Account of the Crisis

I spent a long and very busy day [August 13] in London, and during that day I became convinced that the Government were facing up to the situation and were making a great effort to meet it. The co-operation of the other parties was willingly given to them for that purpose, and I indicated that, so far as our party was concerned, in any effort of that kind they might rely on our support in the House of Commons . . . I certainly was convinced at that time that the Government could fight this matter out by themselves without breaking up. I had no desire to see the government broken up – no one of us had – on this point we would vastly have preferred the Government to have carried on, and we would have assisted them and held ourselves responsible for whatever blame that might be attached to any difficult or unpleasant tasks that might have devolved upon them . . . The last thing I should have thought of would have been to join a National Government.

From Baldwin's speech in the House of Commons, 8 September 1931

C The Crisis Talks at Buckingham Palace

At 10 a.m. the King held a conference at Buckingham Palace at which the Prime Minister, Baldwin and Samuel were present. At the beginning, the King impressed upon them that before they left the Palace some *communiqué* must be issued which would no longer keep the country and the world in suspense. The Prime Minister said that he had the resignation of the Cabinet in his pocket, but the King replied that he trusted there was no question of the Prime Minister's resignation: the leaders of the three parties must get together and come to some arrangement. His Majesty hoped that the Prime Minister, with the colleagues who remained faithful to him, would help in the formation of a National Government, which the King was sure would be supported by the Conservatives and Liberals. The King assured the Prime Minister that, remaining at his post, his position and reputation would be much more enhanced than if he surrendered the government of the country at such a crisis. Baldwin and Samuel said that they were willing to serve under the Prime Minister, and render all help possible to carry on the Government as a National Emergency Government until an emergency bill or bills had been passed by Parliament, which would restore once more British credit and the confidence of foreigners. After that they would expect His Majesty to grant a dissolution. To this course the King agreed. During the Election the National Government would remain in being, though of course each Party would fight the election on its own lines.

Memorandum by George V's Private Secretary, 24 August 1931

D *The Times's* Comment on the Fall of the Labour Government
The Prime Minister and the colleagues of his own party who have followed him deserve in particular unqualified credit, both for the manner in which they took their political lives in their hands by facing and forcing the break-up of the late Cabinet, and for their decision to translate courage in the Cabinet into courage in the country. Their readiness to share the responsibility – honour is perhaps the better word – of carrying through to the end a policy of retrenchment adds enormously to the prospects of its success. No-one henceforth will be able to claim that retrenchment is a class or partisan policy, dictated solely by an unsubstantial panic manufactured by industrial and financial interests. No Conservative or Liberal – it may be earnestly hoped – will deny his share in an arrangement to carry out that part of a national task which all are agreed must come first and cannot be delayed . . .
    It is an interesting, dramatic and logical fact that the Labour Government has fallen in what has always been foreseen to be the acid test of democracy – namely, the capacity of its leaders to tell the people the truth and not to regulate their policy by the votes that it would bring. This is the test which Mr MacDonald, Mr Snowden, and those who supported them have triumphantly survived. That is the test to which their dissentient colleagues have ingloriously succumbed . . .

From *The Times*, 25 August 1931

E The National Government's Appeal to the Electorate
I would warn the electors against being influenced by other considerations than the one issue. That one issue on which you should vote is, as I have stated elsewhere, whether we should have a strong and stable Government in this time of national crisis, or whether we

should hand over the destinies of the nation to men whose conduct in a grave emergency has shown them to be unfitted to be trusted with responsibility. I regret that other issues are being raised in this Election. The position is too serious to have the national unity threatened by divisions on a subject [tariff reform] which is no essential part of the work in front of the National Government.

From an election broadcast by Snowden, 17 October 1931

F An Historian's Verdict
[In the same month [August] the government's unbalanced borrowings to meet the deficit on the Unemployment Insurance Fund precipitated a panic among foreign depositors and an incipient flight from the pound. Amid much confused bandying of figures and waving of depreciated pound notes, and a wholly irrational but rather moving recrudescence of patriotic feeling, a hastily formed coalition government appealed to the country for a 'doctor's mandate' to solve the economic ills under which its people were suffering. It received it with a majority unprecedented in British electoral history. The Socialist and former pacifist Prime Minister, who had abandoned his party at the dictates of his conscience and the Bank of England, was returned to power with a following of 556 members, 472 of whom were Tories.

From A. Bryant: *English Saga, 1940*

Questions

1 From your own knowledge, do you agree with Source A that 'the cause of the trouble was not financial'? **(6 marks)**

2 How far do Sources A–C support or contradict the contention that MacDonald betrayed his party? **(6 marks)**

3 Using Source C and your own knowledge, evaluate George V's role in the political crisis. **(5 marks)**

4 How far do Sources D and E provide an adequate explanation for the landslide victory of the National Government? **(6 marks)**

5 Comment on the content and tone of Source F. **(5 marks)**

6 What difficulties face any historian attempting to construct an objective account of the political crisis of 1931? **(7 marks)**

13 DOLE AND RECOVERY
1931–9

An emergency budget and the abandonment of the Gold Standard soon dealt with the crisis, real or imaginary, of 1931, and the government secured a 'doctor's mandate' for the National Government to continue with more of the same. The introduction of protective tariffs in 1932 seemed a momentous change of policy at the time, but its effect was somewhat disappointing: the Special Areas Act was underfunded and mainly window-dressing; low interest rates could not revive old industries nor provide the mainspring for new ones. Historians hostile to the National Government claim that any recovery before 1939 was despite, rather than because of, government policies while those more favourable to the National Government are usually careful to stress the limited and sometimes unexpected results of government initiatives.

It is not surprising, therefore, that the National Government is remembered for its failures: its failure to deal with the dictators, its failure to rearm in time, its failure to deal with unemployment. And it is remembered even more for its meanness: it is not difficult for its critics to secure the right emotive effect by the careful use of a photograph, or a statistic, or an apt quotation. The 'means test', the 'dole' and appeasement have become the triple indictment against the government of the 1930s.

The decision to restrict unemployment benefit based on contributions to 26 weeks of the year, and to relate unfunded relief to means, derives naturally from the premise that the Unemployment Insurance Fund should be as far as possible self-supporting financially. This was orthodox economics; Keynes was still a voice crying in the wilderness. What was demeaning about the dole was the fact of being in long-term rather than temporary unemployment, and this was too often compounded by an over-strict interpretation of the rules which worsened the misery and degradation of the sufferer. Greater flexibility and greater humanity in the application of the rules by the new Unemployment Assistance Board from 1934 could not take away the despair of long-term unemployment, and the memories of the old system at its worst were never eradicated.

For those out of work, the 1930s meant grinding poverty although not actual starvation; for those in work, improved living standards were a result of falling prices until 1934 and slowly rising wages thereafter. Most historians would argue that the fall in unemployment after 1933 indicated some kind of a recovery, although in 1939 there were still two thirds as many unemployed as there had been in the worst year of 1933. The reasons for this recovery have been much debated. The government's most persistent critics assert that recovery only began with rearmament, although this is difficult to sustain as unemployment had fallen by over 800,000 by the time rearmament began in earnest in 1936. The limited nature of the government's direct measures have been pointed out, but maybe the multiplier effect has been underestimated. The recovery seems to have been at its strongest in house building and in light industry, both of which would have benefitted from low interest rates. Full employment had to wait until the war but, the question of whether it would have been achieved much earlier if Keynesian principles had been put into practice is no longer regarded as purely rhetorical in the present post-Keynesian climate.

A State Intervention

Between the wars, and especially during the 1930s, Britain . . . turned from one of the least into one of the most trustified or controlled economies, and largely through direct government action. It achieved . . . the creation of a government-sponsored monopoly in iron and steel (1932) and a national coal cartel (1936), though success was less in cotton. Equally unthinkable in terms of Victorian capitalism, the government set about regulating prices and output by legal compulsion, notably in agriculture, about one third of whose output was brought into state-sponsored marketing schemes in the early thirties (pigs, bacon, milk, potatoes and hops). By the end of the 1930s some of these schemes had reached the verge of nationalisation – for example of coal royalties (1938) and of British airlines (1939) – while the collapse of industry in the depressed areas had produced at least the principle of a policy for the direct and subsidised fostering of industry by government planning.

From E.J. Hobsbawn: *Industry and Empire* (1968)

B The Unemployment Assistance Board Looks After the Pence

A.K. was a hewer until Hebburn colliery closed, when he got work at the Jarrow shipyard. He is 47 years old which means sentence of economic death on Tyneside if you are once 'out' at that age. He hates enforced idleness and is continually trying for work. He has three children, a boy, aged 16, getting 8s. a week 'sick pay', a boy of 14, chronically rheumatic, and a child of eight. The wife is ailing and bloodless and gets 2s.6d. a week extra allowance from the Unemployment Assistance Board (the UAB). The eldest boy went to work as an errand boy at 6s. a week. He became ill simply because he was not getting enough food to stick the long hours and carry the weights required. The Unemployment Allowance of the family is 35s.6d. Doctor's notes have to be sent in periodically for the mother and sick boys. What is really wrong with all of them is the effect of a long period of semi-starvation. The doctor says so. The 2s.6d extra allowance for the mother is conscientiously spent by the father in milk, eggs and two ounces of fresh butter for her each week. When it does what it is given for and improves the mother's health, then it will be stopped and cannot be given again until the doctor again has to say that the woman is suffering from malnutrition.

From Ellen Wilkinson: *The Town That Was Murdered* (1939)

C The Government Looks After the Pounds

. . . 1931 was a greater watershed than most people realised at the time. Before then, people and politicians alike had been trying to go back to the past. Now they began, albeit in a confused and half-hearted way, to look to the future. In the 'twenties,' few people disputed that Great Britain's troubles had been caused by the upheavals brought by the war, and only the odd prophet like Mosley or Keynes denied that the solution must lie in a return to the self-regulating world economy which had existed before 1914. These notions disappeared with the gold standard. After 1931, Britain had, in effect, a managed currency. Increasingly, she also had a managed economy, where the government takes measures to alter the course of the economy in the direction it thinks fit. Two such measures were the policy of cheap money [low interest rates], claimed as a way of stimulating economic recovery, and the imposition of tariffs, a constraint upon the working of free enterprise . . .

True, Britain's recovery was slow and patchy . . . As late as July 1936 [unemployment] was over one and a half million, while the proportion of insured workers was 12 per cent as against 9.7 per cent in 1929. In the so-called distressed areas – the areas of the traditional staple industries of coal, ship-building, steel and textiles, most of them heavily dependent on traditional export markets – the position was infinitely worse. In 1932, the unemployment percentage in Wales was over 36 per cent, compared with under 14 per cent in London and the South-East. In Merthyr in 1934 over 60 per cent of the insured workers were unemployed; in Jarrow, almost 70 per cent.

From an article by D. Marquand, 1969

D British Economic Statistics for the Mid-1930s

	Unemployed (millions)	Share of world trade (1929 = 100)	Imports (£ millions)
1932	2.85	74.6	710
1933	2.95	75.4	685
1934	2.40	78.2	754
1935	2.29	81.8	797
1936	2.13	85.8	865
1937	1.67	96.8	1048

	Exports (£ millions)	Cost of living (1929 = 100)	Wage rates (1929 = 100)
1932	422	88	96
1933	420	85	95
1934	460	86	96
1935	536	87	97
1936	519	90	99
1937	606	94	103

Adapted from various sources

Questions

1 Is Source A suggesting that government policies during the 1930s were largely successful? Explain your answer. **(9 marks)**

2 'Source B is more of an emotional appeal than an historical statement.' Do you agree? **(4 marks)**

3 From your own knowledge explain:
   a) 'a managed currency' (Source C line 9) **(2 marks)**
   b) why the position was so bad in the 'traditional staple industries' (Source C line 19) **(4 marks)**
   c) the importance of 'cheap money' and 'tariffs' (Source C lines 12 and 14) in bringing about recovery. **(5 marks)**

4 The first paragraph of Source C offers a contrast between the 1920s and 1930s. How far would you support this contrast from your own knowledge and from the evidence of the other sources? **(7 marks)**

5 What are the uses and limitations of Source D as evidence of economic recovery during the mid-1930s? **(8 marks)**

6 Do these sources support the view that the 1930s was a period of severe hardship for considerable numbers of British people? **(6 marks)**

14 THE IMPACT OF WAR ON POLITICS 1939–45

During the First World War there were two significant political events; the formation of the Coalition government in 1915 and the fall of Asquith in 1916. During the Second World War, the parallels of these two events are telescoped into one with the fall of Chamberlain's government in May 1940. Until then Chamberlain had not thought it necessary to include members of other parties in his Cabinet, partly because his government was still nominally National rather than Conservative, partly because Labour would not serve under him anyway, and partly because he did not think that the war was in sufficient crisis for other party participation to be necessary. It was not so much Chamberlain's wartime disasters which brought about his downfall – after all, Britain's situation seemed more desperate several times under Churchill – it was rather his over-confidence and lack of sense of urgency; and possibly he was being punished, in part at any rate, for the pre-war appeasement policies. Nor was Chamberlain's downfall the result of a defeat in Parliament. The abstentions and votes against were significant but not vital. Chamberlain could have carried on, but his authority had been undermined by the defections, and he was persuaded, especially in view of Labour's unwillingness to join a government headed by him, to stand down.

Here there was a similarity with 1922: at that time Lord Curzon and now Lord Halifax seemed the likely candidate for the premiership. But although Halifax was better liked than Curzon, the same objection, that prime ministers should not be in the House of Lords, carried the day, and Churchill was the widely acclaimed choice. Churchill's war leadership was vigorous and seemingly honest. His wartime speeches in 1940 and 1941 promised little but sacrifice, and inspired patriotism. His leadership, decisions and prejudices have earned criticism, some of it trenchant. Yet few at the time disputed that Churchill was the best prime minister we had got, and on balance most historians have agreed.

Despite disasters and mistakes there was little parliamentary criticism of Churchill and his ministers, and the only major motion criticising his conduct of the war was heavily defeated. But there was some political opposition, and the Commonwealth Party captured the dissident vote (and occasionally the seat) when it contested by-elections. Soon after becoming prime minister Churchill took over the leadership of the Conservative Party, thus accepting some responsibility for Conservative pre-war policies, particularly domestic. So when Churchill showed only lukewarm support for the Beveridge Report in the years from 1942, potential voters discriminated even more clearly between Churchill the war hero and Churchill the politician. When the electorate rejected Churchill in 1945 it was the Conservative Party it was rejecting; perhaps Churchill should have devoted more time and effort, especially during the later stages of the war, to giving the Conservative Party a more progressive image. As it was he relied on the gratitude of the nation and his personal charisma, and in the general election of 1945 he was to be bitterly disappointed.

A Low's View of the Crucial Debate

ONE POSITION THAT ISN'T GOING TO BE EVACUATED

Cartoon in the *Evening Standard*, 8 May 1940

B Churchill's Own Account
On the second day, May 8, the debate, although continuing upon an Adjournment Motion, assumed the character of a vote of censure, and Mr Herbert Morrison, in the name of the Opposition, declared their intention to have a vote. The Prime Minister rose again, accepted the challenge, and in an unfortunate passage appealed to his friends to stand by him . . . Mr Lloyd George turned upon Mr Chamberlain.

'It is not a question of who are the Prime Minister's friends. It is a far bigger issue. He has appealed for sacrifice. The nation is prepared for sacrifice so long as it has leadership, so long as the Government show clearly what they are aiming at, and so long as the nation is confident that those who are leading it are doing their best.' [He ended,] *'I say solemnly that the Prime Minister should give an example of sacrifice,*

because there is nothing which can contribute more to victory in this war than that he should sacrifice the seals of office . . .'

I did my very best to regain control of the House for the Government in the teeth of continuous interruption . . . and several times the clamour was such that I could not make myself heard. Yet all the time it was clear that their anger was not directed against me, but at the Prime Minister, whom I was defending to the utmost of my ability and without regard for any other considerations.

From W.S. Churchill: *The Second World War* (1948)

C Macmillan Recalls

During the evening [of 8 May] I saw Churchill in the smoking-room . . . I wished him luck, but added that I hoped his speech would not be too convincing. 'Why not?' he asked. 'Because', I replied 'we must have a new Prime Minister, and it must be you.' He answered gruffly that he had signed on for the voyage and would stick to the ship. But I don't think he was angry with me.

[*And the following day . . .*]

Rumour was rife. Some said that Chamberlain would stay. Others declared that Halifax would succeed him. Others again believed that nothing could resist Churchill's claims. It was thought that the Labour chiefs leaned towards Halifax. Churchill's long and active career had brought him many enemies as well as devoted friends.

From H. Macmillan: *The Blast of War* (1967)

D Great Events

The morning of May 10 dawned and with it the news . . . that Holland and Belgium were both invaded . . . At eleven o'clock I was again summoned to Downing Street by the Prime Minister. There once more I found Lord Halifax. We took our seats at the table opposite Mr Chamberlain. He told us that he was satisfied that it was beyond his power to form a National Government. The response he had received from the Labour leaders left him in no doubt of this. The question was therefore whom should he advise the King to send for . . .

I have had many interviews in my public life, and this was certainly the most important. Usually I talk a great deal but on this occasion I was silent . . . As I remained silent a very long pause ensued . . . Then at length Halifax spoke. He said that he felt that his position as a peer, out of the House of Commons, would make it very difficult for him to discharge the duties of Prime Minister in a war like this. He would be held responsible for everything, but would not have the power to guide the assembly upon whose confidence the life of every Government depended. He spoke for some minutes in this sense, and by the time he had finished it was clear that the duty would fall upon me . . .

From W.S. Churchill: *The Second World War* (1948)

Questions

1 Study Source A.
  a) Using your own knowledge, explain the reference to '8 years of dithering'. **(4 marks)**
  b) How significant do you regard (i) Baldwin's portrait on the wall and (ii) the absence of important members of the Cabinet from the group on the right of the cartoon? **(5 marks)**
  c) What do you consider to be the main aim of the cartoonist in drawing this cartoon? **(4 marks)**

2 Using your own knowledge, explain why Churchill is 'defending the Prime Minister to the utmost of my ability' in Source B. **(5 marks)**

3 Was Macmillan correct in saying (Source C) that Churchill had 'many enemies?' use your own knowledge to develop your answer. **(6 marks)**

4 Explain Churchill's silence in Source D (line 11). **(3 marks)**

5 From the sources and your own knowledge, consider the view that Churchill's intention from the beginning of the debate was to take Chamberlain's place. **(8 marks)**

15 THE IMPACT OF WAR ON SOCIETY 1939–45

'Total war' is the term often used to describe the Second World War and to distinguish it from its predecessors. In so far as it implies massive civilian involvement, and a blurring of the distinction between armed forces as combatants and civilians as non-combatants, the term has validity. But it needs to be used with caution. Until June 1940 British civilians were barely touched by the war: most rationing and the worst air-raids were still to come, and the mobilisation of labour was as yet in its infancy. Even when the war was at its height British civilians were spared the horrors that were endured by the populations of much of mainland Europe and of parts of Asia.

Most Britons 'carried on' despite the war, but it had its immediacy in many different ways. The bombings, although only killing 65,000 civilians, destroyed or damaged two in every seven houses; news on the radio usually anticipated the newspapers by several hours, and live speeches and action were much more effective than print; shortages and rationing made almost every meal a test of ingenuity; travel by public transport was essential in the absence of private cars (though long journeys were frowned on as unpatriotic and when undertaken were often hazardous) and Civil Defence, voluntary organisations, the Home Guard and the Land Army were among the many areas to which almost all active adults devoted part-time or full-time energies. It might be possible to get away from the war for a few hours on a quiet afternoon in the country, but for the vast majority of the population the war was an ever-present determining factor in both work and leisure.

State regulation and intervention took place on a more massive scale, and were better organised than during the First World War. The war effort was run under a system of dilute State socialism, legislated for by a largely Conservative Parliament. Women were not only expected to work, they were conscripted to do so, and the war did at least undermine the prejudice, strong in many professions, against the employment of married women. The mixing of classes and the weakening of social barriers was a positive side-effect of evacuation, bombing and labour conscription, even if the evacuees' table manners and other habits were not always fully appreciated by some of the middle-class families on whom they had been billeted. Class prejudices were not, of course, eradicated, although domestic service became a casualty in common with much that was not vital to the war effort.

In the darkest days of the war, from the summer of 1940 until the autumn of 1942, war camaraderie united the country behind Churchill in pugnacious defiance and a determination, if necessary, to fight to the end. When the war news brightened there was widespread consensus not only that war should never recur, but that this war must lead to a better life. Beveridge came at the right moment, and the 1945 general election result was both a decisive rejection of the 1930s and an emphatic demand for a better future.

A The Need for an Increased Labour Force

We have to make a huge expansion, especially of those capable of performing skilled or semi-skilled operations. Here we must specially count for aid and guidance upon our Labour colleagues and trade union leaders. I can speak with some knowledge about this, having presided over the former Ministry of Munitions in its culminating phase. Millions of new workers will be needed, and more than a million women must come boldly forward into our war industries – into the shell plants, the munition works, and into the aircraft factories. Without this expansion of labour and without allowing the women of Britain to enter the struggle as they desire to do, we should fail utterly to bear our fair share of the burden which Britain and France have assumed.

From a speech by W.S. Churchill, 27 January 1940

B Civilian Hardships
(i) 15 November 1940

Poor, poor Coventry! the attack is described on the wireless as a 'vicious attack against an open town comparable to one of the worst raids on London, and the damage very considerable'. The casualties are in the neighbourhood of a thousand, and the beautiful fourteenth-century cathedral is destroyed . . . The Curtises say their Works is burned down and we hear of fires spreading because of the lack of water, as the water main is damaged. One cannot judge the reports as there is no telephone communication with Leamington, Coventry and several places around. Often reports are grossly exaggerated and one dare not accept them.

(ii) 18 July 1941

In Leamington this morning we had a good deal to do and shopping takes a long time. People take their rations books to the shops and they have to have the coupons cancelled as well as being served with bits of this and that.

Red currants are 2s.6d. a pound, cherries 4s.6d., dessert gooseberries 3s.6d., and the greengrocer said 'They're not worth it! Wouldn't pay it' as he emptied them from a basket to a punnet. Potatoes are very scarce and when I asked if I could have two pounds, the greengrocer's wife said 'Have three'. So I did. Life is certainly strange now, with coupons for clothes, and very ordinary commodities like potatoes kept in the shops for regular customers only!

(iii) 9 September 1942

A petrol coupon arrived this morning for land-girl work, so we both took the car out – the first time since 28th June – and it was lovely to be in it again. I have written and offered my services and the car for the WVS [Women's Voluntary Service] pool, whereby one is sent on a job occasionally and petrol is provided. *Anything* to get a legitimate run in the car these days!

From *Mrs Milburn's Diaries*

C And More Hardship

(i) 2 February 1942

A woman from Middlesbrough was fined 10s. after being found guilty of wasting food. The court heard she threw buttered slices of bread into the garden. It was the first charge of its kind in the town under the Waste of Food Order, 1940.

(ii) 4 August 1942

Seven people have been killed and serious damage done to Middlesbrough railway station in an air raid . . . The raid comes eight days after Middlesbrough's worst attack of the war when waves of aircraft dropped incendiary bombs in a bid to bring blitz-style destruction to the area. In all 16 people died and more than 80 were injured. Many houses and business premises were destroyed but the raid failed to bring large-scale fire-damage. That was partly due to the efforts of civil defence volunteers, and partly to individuals.

From the *Middlesbrough Evening Gazette*

D A Woman Takes Charge, a Daughter's Recollection

We were all awake as we couldn't sleep and suddenly we heard this plane coming down. We all got up and tore back the curtains on the shelter door to look. Not only was there a plane coming down, but a parachute too. He floated down and landed on the roof of the brick shelter next door. It was a German pilot, so my mother said 'There's nobody about, so I suppose I'll have to do it'. She grabbed a pitchfork and a broom and marched out to the garden next door. In a loud voice she said 'You're under arrest. Put your hands up!' She was fantastic. So he surrendered and gave my mother his parachute. She quickly threw it into the air raid shelter before the Home Guard came to take him away. The next day she dyed the 'chute yellow and two weeks later my sister and I went off to school in bright yellow dresses.

From B. Wicks: *Waiting For The All Clear* (1990)

E The Role of Women Assessed by an Historian

. . . In fact conscription played a very minor role in the changes in women's employment during the war. In practice only single women of the age group 19–24 were called up, and they were given the choice of serving in the Women's Auxiliary Services, in Civil Defence, or in certain specified forms of civilian employment. At the end of the war there were rather fewer than half a million women enrolled in the WRNS (Women's Royal Naval Service), the ATS (Auxiliary Territorial Service), and the WAAF (Women's Auxiliary Air Force), and the larger proportion of these were volunteers not conscripts. In civilian trades women's employment expanded most noticeably in light engineering and in agriculture. By late 1944 48 per cent of all Civil Service employees were women, and women's employment in commerce had almost doubled to 62 per cent of the total number employed. There was nothing quite like the 'Votes for Women' cry of pre-1914 days, but two other causes did receive a boost from the war experience: equal pay, and the movement against the marriage bar still maintained in many of the professions.

From an article by A. Marwick, 1969

Questions

1 Does the evidence of these sources suggest that the civilian population suffered severely during the war? Explain your answer. **(7 marks)**

2 How reliable as evidence do you regard Sources B and D? **(5 marks)**

3 Is it possible from these sources to agree that Britain made full use of the female population in the war effort? **(6 marks)**

4 What other evidence would an historian need for a detailed study of the role of women during the Second World War? **(7 marks)**

A Capitalism Under Threat

A WAITING GAME.

LABOUR PARTY (*to* CAPITALIST). "THAT'S ALL RIGHT, GUV'NOR. I WON'T LET HIM BITE YOU. (*Aside, to dog.*) WAIT TILL YOU'VE GROWN A BIT, MY BEAUTY, AND YOU'LL GET A BIGGER MOUTHFUL!"

From *Punch*, 29 January 1908

B Ulster and Other Troubles

A NATION OF FIRE-EATERS.

PEACEFUL TEUTON. "HIMMEL! THEY HAVE ALL THOSE ARMIES! AND THE FATHER LAND HAS ONLY ONE!"

From *Punch*, 3 December 1913

C The Power Struggle, 1916

A NON-PARTY MANDATE.

John Bull. "I DON'T CARE WHO LEADS THE COUNTRY SO LONG AS HE LEADS IT TO VICTORY."

-From *Punch*, December 1916

D Punch's View of the British Socialists Who Had Gone to Stockholm to Talk Peace

THE REAL VOICE OF LABOUR.

TOMMY. "SO YOU'RE GOING TO STOCKHOLM TO TALK TO FRITZ, ARE YOU? WELL, I'M GOING BACK TO FRANCE TO *FIGHT* HIM."

From *Punch,* 15 August 1917

E In Praise of the Minister of Munitions

DELIVERING THE GOODS.

From *Punch*, 1915

F Punch's Own Red Scare, 1924 General Election

ON THE LOAN TRAIL.

[In a document just disclosed by the British Foreign Office (apparently after considerable delay), M. ZINOVIEFF, a member of the Bolshevist Dictatorship, urges the British Communist Party to use "the greatest possible energy" in securing the ratification of Mr. MacDonald's Anglo-Russian Treaty, in order to facilitate a scheme for "an armed insurrection" of the British proletariat.]

From *Punch*, 29 October 1924

G A Cartoon Comment on the Aftermath of the General Strike

THE MAN IN CONTROL.

JOHN BULL (*to the Pilot*). "YOU'VE GOT US THROUGH THAT FOG SPLENDIDLY."
MR. BALDWIN (*sticking quietly to his job*). "TELL ME ALL ABOUT THAT WHEN WE'RE PAST THESE ROCKS."

From *Punch*, May 1926

H Another Cartoon Comment on the Aftermath of the General Strike

RAMSAY: '*Call yerself a showman; why, yer couldn't run a whelk stall.*'
STANLEY: '*Well, and who wants to run a whelk stall?*'

From the *Daily Express*, 17 May 1926

I Wooing the New Voters

THE DARK HORSE

From the *Daily Express*, 12 October 1927

J MacDonald Does His Best

THE MASTER CHEMIST.

PROFESSOR MacDONALD. "NOW IF ONLY THESE RATHER ANTAGONISTIC ELEMENTS WILL BLEND AS I HOPE, WE'LL HAVE A REAL NATIONAL ELIXIR."

From *Punch*, August 1931

K The 'Bloodthirsty' Labour Party Expels MacDonald and Thomas and Looks for More Victims

From the *Daily Express*, September 1931

L Bevin's newspaper urges workers not to be taken in by Lloyd George's tricks

LLOYD GEORGE: '*Let me give you a "New Deal" with these?*'
CHORUS FROM CARRIAGE: '*No thanks. We're having a "Square Deal" with these cards and on* THIS TABLE.'

From *The Record*, February 1935

M Beveridge to the Rescue

From the *Daily Herald*, 2 December 1942

Questions

1 Identify which of the cartoons are hostile to the Labour Party.

(6 marks)

2 Identify which of the cartoons support progressive causes. **(3 marks)**

3 Examine the techniques used by the cartoonists in Sources A–M in making their point. **(7 marks)**

4 Choose any four of Sources A–M and for each explain:
   a) the message of the source;
   b) at whom it was probably aimed;
   c) how you would evaluate its impact. **(4 × 6 marks)**

5 'As all cartoonists are presenting a point of view they distort the truth and their work is therefore of little value to historians.' Do you agree? You should refer to the sources in your answer. **(10 marks)**

17 HISTORIOGRAPHY

The more recent the historical period the more likely that historians' views will be coloured by their personal prejudices. Modern historians, unlike those of the nineteenth century, do not claim infallibility for their opinions and judgements, but they do not always succeed in offering a balanced view, and students should read widely and attempt to make their own assessment. No-one can judge historical questions with absolute impartiality, but at least it is worthwhile attempting to achieve it.

Some of the areas of controversy in the period 1900–1945 have been touched on earlier in the book. No complete consensus can be expected in judging key personalities of the period, and motive is always more difficult to evaluate than ability and achievement. Issues such as the decline of the Liberal Party, the need for a national government in 1931, the extent and nature of hardship in the 1930s, the cause and extent of economic recovery by 1939, the importance of the world wars in emancipating women – are none of them capable of a simple interpretation, but they offer fruitful lines of investigation to the young historian. Much can be learnt by comparing the approaches of different historians, and seeing how effectively they make use of the evidence. The three extracts which follow, in which three historians attempt to assess Lloyd George, are typical of the difficulty in reaching consensus about major political figures since 1900.

A The Tragedy of Lloyd George

Lloyd George's Liberalism was a permanent phenomenon: whatever he was during this period, he was never a conservative. His Liberalism had many constant features that persistently recurred – its link with the chapels, with rural radicalism, with the popular press, and with the vital national culture of Wales. But his Liberalism, equally, bore only an intermittent and erratic relationship to the Liberal Party as such. Nor did Lloyd George trouble unduly to identify himself with that party. His instinctive democracy, his hatred of privilege, his roots in the warm chapel-bound populism of his native Wales conflicted with his urge for supreme executive power, the kind of instinctive reaction that made him ultimately more at home with imperialists like Milner and Kerr than with individualistic Welsh 'pro-Boers'. The democrat and the dictator were at odds with one another. During the period up to 1914, indeed, it seemed that these rival aspects of Lloyd George's character could be reconciled . . . Lloyd George's own career showed how a traditional

Liberal's concern with social equality could be harmonised with a new
Liberal's search for economic justice, how the basic Gladstonian urge
for greater democracy could be extended . . . But in the event, the
harmony of the old Liberalism and the new depended too much on their
identification with Lloyd George himself. As a result, confronted by the
obscene tragedy of the First World War, which mocked at every moral
value which Liberalism embodied, Lloyd George's own manoeuvres
were not only damaging to the Liberal Party as an organisation, but fatal
for the union of the various strands which it contained. As a result, after
1918, the Liberal Party without Lloyd George was an outdated,
backward-looking movement which had lost contact with the new
Liberalism of the pre-war period. Lloyd George, without the Liberal
Party, was a volatile, erratic individual, full of radical impulses which the
harsh facts of the Coalition (created by his own 'coupon election')
forced him to suppress.

From K.O. Morgan: *The Age of Lloyd George* (1971)

B Lloyd George The Rebel

When Maynard Keynes wrote of Lloyd George that he was 'rooted in
nothing' he was probably as near to the truth about him as anyone is
likely to get; the phrase helps to explain the difficulty of arriving at a
consistent opinion about him. Lloyd George's origins were in the rural
Radicalism of Nonconformist west Wales, and this is enough in itself to
explain his lifelong indifference to English traditions and institutions . . .
As a rural Radical, he hated the English governing class and disliked and
feared the industrial working-class. His Radicalism did not, of course,
constitute much more than a state of mind once he had arrived in
politics. He had little then but his capacity to speak and to act; but with
few real values to give coherence either to what he said or to what he
did. Lloyd George rarely saw anything but given problems and the need
to solve them; for him, a problem had no history and no context but the
immediate situation . . .
  Not only was he rooted in nothing; he refused even to be grafted.
Almost all rebel politicans who work within, or indeed against, the
English tradition, become in the end assimiliated to it, whether their
origins are in Clydeside, Lossiemouth, Lambeth, or Allahabad, but no
man seems to have been more thoroughly insulated against the subtle
attractions of the English way of life than Lloyd George . . . He wanted
the reality of power; for its trappings he cared nothing. For this, he was
never forgiven; to men brought up in the English public school and
university tradition to be careless about the trivialities of public ritual
was to be sacrilegious.
  Equally un-English was his passion for speed. The pitch and moment
of his acts were not to be sicklied o'er with the pale cast of official or

expert dubieties. He always sought the fastest means to the quickest decision . . . If there had to be advisers, they must be quick-witted, highly articulate people of his own choice. This explains why he was opposed with such malevolence not only from the Tory back-benches but from the clubs where Civil Servants and academics congregated.

From L.C.B. Seaman: *Post-Victorian Britain, 1902–1951* (1966)

C Lloyd George Admired

'L.G.' was the sort of man people admired or loathed; there were no half measures either in him or in people's opinion of him. He was above all things clever, with a mind extraordinarily quick and versatile. With this went a buoyancy and courage that were almost brazen, a tendency to ruthlessness and tyrannical behaviour, and a readiness of decision and action which terrified some, but carried others to heights they would never have scaled alone. With him, the end was more important than the means; his methods were personal, improvised, and on occasions unscrupulous; he liked to cut through the rules. There was also a sort of sixth-sense, a 'medium-like sensibility' to persons around him, a personal charm and intuition which anticipated thoughts and saw the quickest way to persuade an adversary or to tackle a problem. He was a genius with a double dose of everything, good and bad. He could do as well with his left hand as his right. Yet it was wrong to deduce from all this as Keynes did, that he was 'rooted in nothing' and without principles. A deep patriotism was his, and a hatred of oppression. 'The volatility of his methods', observed Harold Nicolson,' concealed the rock-like immobility of his aims.' . . . Winston Churchill who admitted him alone as master – in itself a tremendous tribute – summed him up when he wrote: 'He was the greatest master of the art of getting things done and of putting things through that I ever knew; in fact no British politican in my day has possessed half his competence as a mover of men and affairs'.

From C.L. Mowat: *Britain Between the Wars 1918–1940* (1955)

Questions

1 Identify the areas of agreement and the areas of disagreement between these three sources. **(7 marks)**

2 'Because the author of Source A is specifically concerned with Lloyd George as leader of a political party, his judgement is the most critical of the three'. Do you agree? **(8 marks)**

3 Assess the contribution of any historian with whom you are familiar to your understanding of any controversial British historical problem within the period 1900 to 1945. **(10 marks)**

18 DEALING WITH
EXAMINATION QUESTIONS

Specimen Source Question Answer

(See page 57)

1 Was Ramsay MacDonald arguing for a coalition government in Source A? Explain your answer. **(5 marks)**

It could be argued that a leader of a minority government, aware of the ability of the opposition's power to bring down his government at any time, would appeal in this way for a breathing space. There is nothing specific in this speech would could be interpreted as a move for coalition. Indeed MacDonald is quite specific that party principles must not be abandoned. But he may have been looking for the co-operation of other parties in securing non-controversial legislation as the final sentence suggests. It is, however, just conceivable that he could have been testing the water: politicians need to prepare themselves for every eventuality.

2a) Is Source B an effective defence to the charge that the Liberals were keeping MacDonald in power? **(5 marks)**

It might have impressed the Liberal Conference: it was Lloyd George at his most alluring and at his most devious. He was trying to obscure the issue with an unsuitable analogy. He seems to be suggesting that politicians should not stick to their chosen path, including presumably their principles, but should weave right or left as occasion demands. He hints that sticking to liberalism would lead to disaster of Titanic-like proportions, and would in fact be doing the work of the Tories. This is a typical Lloyd George *tour de force:* argument is conspicuously absent.

2b) What was Lloyd George hinting at (Source B) in suggesting that some Liberals may 'have already made arrangements to be picked up'? **(3 marks)**

In defending his policy Lloyd George is attempting to isolate its opponents from the rest of the party. Thus he hints that some of the policy opponents are planning to avoid the disaster of withdrawing backing from the Labour government, by their intention to defect to another party, presumably to the Tories.

3 Using only the evidence of Source D, explain the likely reasons why the Labour government chose to ignore the Report of the Royal Commission. **(5 marks)**

The Fund was shown to be financially unsound, but the three remedies of the Commission would all clash with Labour's image as the protector of the weakest in the community. The limiting of benefit to 26 weeks would throw long-term unemployed onto the mercies of the Poor Law; the increase in contributions would not be popular and Labour could well have preferred a non-contributory scheme anyway; and proposals for reduction of benefit would worsen the condition of those least able to cope. Moreover Labour may have hoped that the proposals of the final Report would be less stringent, or that economic conditions might, by then, have begun to improve, making urgent action on the Fund less necessary.

4a) How does source F reveal the prejudices of its authors?   **(6 marks)**

The authors are obviously left-wing and intolerant of Snowden and MacDonald. The theme is the government's acceptance that the poor, and by implication the poor alone, should be made to carry the burden of expenditure reduction. The tone is disapproving and is supported by such careful choice of words and phrases as 'clamoured for', and 'badgered' – which powerfully support the thesis of a government under pressure, and 'as many as possible' and 'any sort' which offer a little exaggeration to heighten the effect. The juxtaposition of the maintenance of the Gold Standard, possibly a legitimate government aim, with the maintenance of the 'profit system', which was certainly not an aim a socialist government could defend, is a shrewd way of undermining the government. The use of inverted commas to enclose 'sound finance' implies disapproval of Snowden, and there is an intended touch of irony at the end in the requirement of a socialist government to 'enjoy the fullest confidence of the capitalist class'.

4b) Do any of the other sources give justification to the view put forward in Source F? Explain your answer.   **(4 marks)**

Sources A–C, in suggesting the idea of party co-operation, might support the implication of Source F that Labour was prepared to abandon its principles, but only in the most general way. Source D indicates that the government was under some pressure, but not that the government was prepared to give in to it. Some pressure is also implied in the rising unemployment figures in Source E. However, nothing in these sources justifies the response to the pressures which is asserted in Source F.

5 Using sources D–F and your own knowledge, explain why the second Labour government found unemployment so difficult a problem to tackle.   **(7 marks)**

Source E shows the rapidly rising number of the unemployed. The government was unable, in view of its minority in Parliament, to tackle unemployment with socialist measures. And it was boxed into a corner by its acceptance of orthodox economic and financial theories. Thus the deficit in the Unemployment Fund (Source D) would add to the government's borrowing needs, making a balanced budget more difficult to achieve, and the failure to understand or accept the Keynsian approach meant that the government did not have the option of spending itself out of recession and thus reducing unemployment. But even if Keynes's theories had been accepted and put into practice it is arguable whether they would have worked. They might have given a boost to the new industries of the south and midlands which did not need one, and done nothing for the structural unemployment of the traditional industries of the north which, apart from textiles, were virtually incapable of expansion. Abandoning the Gold Standard might have reduced banking uncertainty and restored some business confidence with a possible marginal effect on unemployment, but Snowden told his colleagues that that option was not available. So the government could only hope that somehow, out of a political consensus, a solution to a seemingly intractable problem would miraculously appear. Source F, whose authors had the benefit of hindsight, is a caustic comment on the government's dilemma.

Approaching Essay Questions

The key to writing successful history essays must always be in the last resort the ability to achieve relevance; in other words you must answer the particular question set. Relevance is worth more than length or a mass of detail. Accurate knowledge is also important, but only if it is employed as evidence to back up a particular argument. Narrative, without analysis, or prepared answers to a topic which do not meet the requirements of the particular title set, are probably the commonest failings of examination answers. Conversely, the best answers are often concise, always relevant, analytical, and show evidence of wide and thoughtful reading. Your command of the English language is not being tested specifically, but you must be able to present your arguments coherently, logically and effectively.

Plan your essays. Break the question down into its key components. What are the key phrases or words in the question? Give your essays a shape: an introduction which will introduce the main argument and possibly indicate how you hope to approach it; a logical main body, written in paragraphs (sometimes ignored by students!); and a conclusion which does not repeat the bulk of your essay but neatly draws together the threads. Other issues such as style and use of quotations are also important if you wish to write lucidly and well. As with most things in life, essay writing usually improves with practice.

In most of the history essays you encounter, you will be asked to evaluate a statement or quotation, or answer a direct question. There are usually different approaches you may adopt: therefore 'model' answers must be treated with caution. It is, for example, quite in order to approach a controversial issue by considering evidence which supports different sides of an argument, without necessarily coming down on one side of a particular interpretation. On the other hand, it is equally acceptable to argue a particular viewpoint, provided you can produce supporting evidence. Credit will usually be given if you show relevant knowledge of contemporary and/or more recent sources.

Every essay will have a *theme*, i.e a central historical topic, and a *focus*, i.e. the specific analysis required. Thus in the question 'How far did the Liberal governments, 1906–14, have a deliberate social policy?' the theme is the Liberal governments, but the focus on which the effectiveness of the answer hinges is the extent to which the Liberal governments had a specific social policy. A narrative of their achievements will not provide the analysis required.

It is vitally important to notice the theme/focus nature of essay questions. Some students seize on the theme only and ignore the focus, producing answers which are often largely irrelevant or only remotely relevant. If they hit the target they usually do so by accident rather than by design. A useful test is to cover up the title of an essay written some time ago and see if you can work out an approximation of the title. If you can identify only the theme, but not the focus, then your essay was not a particularly strong one.

There are books available which deal in some depth with issues such as analytical reading, question analysis and essay-writing. Students may well find any of the following useful:

C. Brasher: *The Young Historian* (OUP 1970)
J. Cloake, V. Crinnon and S. Harrison: *The Modern History Manual* (Framework Press 1987)
J. Fines: *Studying To Succeed – History at A Level and Beyond* (Longman 1986)

Most essays fall into clearly defined categories:

'How far' or 'To what extent'?
This sort of question requires a balanced approach, with consideration of points both ways. If, for example, in answering 'How far was X concerned to promote social welfare in his domestic policies?' you asserted that all his policies were so geared, you would surely be wrongly ignoring those aspects of his domestic policy which were not devoted to social welfare. In the end you are looking for a balanced judgement.

'Why'/'Account for'
These are *reasons* questions, and are some of the most straightforward and easy to tackle, but beware of the elementary mistake of confusing 'Account for' with 'Give an account of': it is the worst possible technique to present

a narrative and expect the reader or examiner to deduce or infer his or her own reasons from it. It is also very important to develop your own GCSE training in the effective handling of causation: you should arrange and develop your reasons in a planned sequence so that the points are effectively linked and follow on logically from the one to the next.

Comparison questions

These are less common than formerly but still appear in different guises. It might be a comparison of two politicians or statesmen, or it might be a comparison of policies. Whichever it is, a point by point comparison is far more effective than treating the two (or more) to be compared one after the other.

Judgement questions

These are very popular questions with examiners. A judgement on some person or event is presented for you to support or otherwise. As these are also popular with GCSE examiners you should already have some experience of them, and be familiar with the necessary basic techniques. In nearly all instances a balanced approach will be needed. You may be able to support the judgement up to a point but will have reservations which you must develop. Perhaps the judgement is largely unsupportable – then you will have to prove it to be so. Never assume that you are expected to give a judgement unqualified support, although in the end your answer may turn out that way. But remember that in History, categorical statements are nearly always capable of some challenge.

The following list of essay titles on Britain 1900–1945 includes analysis of type, suggestions (no more than suggestions!) on how to approach them, plus a specimen answer. Use them as part of your course or for examination practice.

Possible Essay Titles

1 Sydney Webb in 1901 called the Liberal Party obsolescent. How far was this a reasonable judgement of the state of the Liberal Party in 1901?

(See specimen answer on page 101)

2 How far was Conservative disunity the reason for the Conservative general election defeat of 1906?

The theme is the election of 1906, and the focus is the extent to which Conservative disunity (i.e. over tariff reform) contributed to the Conservative defeat. It is important to remember that disunity was not the only reason for the defeat. Other causes: Liberal revival and programme, the fading of Boer War jingoism, the effects of the Education

Act, Chinese 'slavery', Taff Vale – all need attention, and the importance of Conservative disunity as a cause of defeat should be judged in the context of the other reasons for it.

3 Why did the Liberal government encounter so many domestic difficulties from 1909 to 1914?

The domestic difficulties form the theme and the focus is on the reasons for them. Thus narratives of suffragettes, strikes, Lords controversy and Home Rule (domestic in this context) should be avoided. Concentrate on explanation – suffragette impatience with the lack of progress towards the enfranchisement of women, the growing power of the trade unions (Trades Disputes Act 1906) and the need to maintain and improve standards of living against a background of slowly rising prices. The Lords controversy needs to be explained not in terms of what happened in the years 1909–11, but how it arose, and it can easily be linked to the revival of the Irish Question. In considering why they faced so many problems all at once the Liberals were not just unfortunate; it could be argued that the difficulties were exacerbated by inept handling (the suffragettes), by deliberate policy (the House of Lords), and by too simplistic an approach (Ireland).

4 Why was the constitutional crisis of 1909–1911 so difficult to resolve?

The crisis is the theme and it is important to avoid narrative and concentrate on the focus, which is concerned with the difficulties in ending it. The importance to both sides of the constitutional issues involved, the determination of Liberals like Lloyd George to secure permanent victory without compromise, Conservative fear of unchallengeable social legislation and such contentious policies as Home Rule, the change of monarch, the failure of the constitutional conference, the Ditchers – all provide useful material for argument.

5 Why did the Conservative Party survive the electoral defeats of the early twentieth century?

The theme is the Conservative Party (not the 1906 election) and the focus is on explaining its survival. It would be sensible to begin with the 1906 election to show that the magnitude of the Conservative defeat was brought about by a unique combination of circumstances, unlikely to be repeated, and that the 1910 results were arguably more typical. An analysis of conservatism, its appeal and its adaptability could lead to a consideration of the Liberal split in 1916, the remarkable upsurge of conservatism in the Coupon Election, and conservatism (rather than liberalism) being the natural home of those who disliked the socialism of the rapidly growing Labour Party. It might be argued that the enfranchisement of women, begun in 1918, was a boost to Conservative voting strength.

6 Assess the effects of the First World War on British politics.

Here the theme is British politics during and after the First World War. The war is not the theme, but the focus is the *effect* of the war on politics. Narratives of the war will be irrelevant, and narratives of British politics from 1914 into the 1920s will only be relevant where the effect of war on politics is dealt with. The Liberal split in 1916, and its widening in 1918 with the Maurice debate will certainly be central to the argument. It will be necessary to consider the widespread view that the decline of the Liberal Party only really began with this split. Lloyd George's failure to create his own party, and thus his dependence on Conservative support led to the Conservatives being the real victors of the Coupon Election and the Liberals the main losers. But do not ignore other issues. Henderson's removal from Lloyd George's Cabinet in 1917, and Labour as the largest opposition party in 1918 were important for the growth and independence of the Labour Party. Finally, the personal friendships and animosities arising from wartime politics were to have repercussions, especially in 1922, but even beyond.

7 'The best that could be obtained under the circumstances'. Is this a fair verdict on the Irish settlement of 1922?

This is a judgement question, and not an invitation to pour out narrative on Ireland from 1918–22. The theme is the Irish settlement, but the focus is on whether it was the best obtainable at the time. The circumstances should be specifically related to post–1918 and the usual lengthy background introductions should be avoided. A number of factors could be considered: the commitment of the Sinn Fein Irish leaders to independence and their unwillingness to compromise, the commitment of Northern Irish Protestants to remain in the Union, Lloyd George's dependence on Conservative support and Conservative dislike for Home Rule, let alone independence. The significance of the Government of Ireland Act in preparing the way for partition, and the skill of Lloyd George in getting agreement, whether by promises, threats or both, will need to be discussed. The compromise of 1922 was accepted with the greatest reluctance by all concerned. *Was* there any better alternative? And could any other politician or statesmen have done better than Lloyd George?

8 Why was there so dramatic a decline in the fortunes of the Liberal Party between 1918 and 1931?

The theme is the Liberal Party and the focus is on the reasons for its decline. Narrative must be avoided: a good answer will investigate the

Liberal split and its effect on the Coupon Election of 1918, the rise of Labour as the party of radicalism, the Coalition and its end in 1922, the failure of Lloyd George and Asquith to settle their differences except briefly in 1923, and their disagreement over the General Strike. The party's lack of an effective programme in the early 1920s (except for free trade), its responsibility for maintaining Labour in power and for removing Labour from power, and the effect of both of these on the electorate will need to be discussed, as will the Depression and the formation of the National Government which arguably isolated and split the Liberal Party further. Dangerfield's views (*The Strange Death of Liberal England*) are no longer acceptable without qualification.

9 In the general election of 1906 the Conservative Party won only 157 seats in the House of Commons. In the 1922 election it won 347. How do you account for this transformation in Conservative fortunes.

The theme is the Conservative Party (not the two elections) and the focus is the explanation of the Conservative revival. This can partly be explained by events outside the party; the divisions in the Liberal Party, the quirkish allocation of the coupon in 1918, the splitting of the radical vote between Liberal and Labour, discontent with Lloyd George, and the new female voters. But how far the result of 1906 underestimated the strength of the country's conservatism, and how far the party was reinvigorated from within, need to be considered.

10 Why did Lloyd George's political influence decline after 1922?

The theme is Lloyd George but the focus is on the decline of his influence. Do not write political narratives of Lloyd George's career after 1922, or even worse, of his career before that. The obvious starting point will be an *explanation* of his political dominance 1918–22 if the decline is to be effectively pointed. Even in this dominance there were intrinsic weaknesses; the Coalition MPs were mostly Conservative, Lloyd George had encountered difficulties in carrying out his policies, and his personal weaknesses seemed to be typified by the Honours Scandal. The so-called Liberal reunion of 1923 did not really heal the Liberal split, and the remainder of the essay should be concerned with the replacement of the Liberals by Labour as the alternative to the Conservatives, suspicion of Lloyd George in all parties, the new Liberal split in 1931, and Lloyd George's attitude towards and exclusion from the successive national governments of the 1930s.

11 Compare Asquith and Lloyd George as politicians and statesmen.

Note the double focus here on 'politicians' and 'statesmen'. Devoting the first half of the essay to one man and the second half to the other is poor technique. It should not be too difficult to present a point by point comparison of the two men whose careers were so often parallel. It would be useful to establish your own idea of the distinction between politicans and statesmen.

12 Was the failure of the General Strike a triumph for Baldwin?

The theme is the General Strike and the focus is on whether its failure was a triumph for Baldwin. Here the conflicting views of Baldwin will determine your answer. If, from the autumn of 1925 he deliberately set out to provoke a general strike in order to outwit the TUC, then its failure can only have been a triumph for him. If, on the other hand, Baldwin is seen as the conciliator, the man who wished to be trusted, the man who tried to prevent the strike but failed, then 'triumph' is a questionable verdict. Certainly right-wing opinion gave Baldwin the credit for the strike's failure, but Baldwin did not trumpet his victory, and the strike's failure made it more difficult for him to resist anti-trade union legislation in 1927 than when he had previously opposed it in 1925. In the long-term, too, triumph is questionable. The defeat of Baldwin's party in the 1929 election, and Labour bitterness against some of his colleagues (which made things difficult in 1931) suggest that there was some hollowness about this triumph.

13 Can the lack of socialism in the domestic policies of the two Labour governments, 1923–4 and 1929–31, be attributed entirely to their lack of a majority in Parliament?

The domestic policies of the two governments provide the theme, and the focus is the extent to which lack of a parliamentary majority explains their limitations. You might, of course, argue about what is meant by socialist in relation to what was actually achieved. The word 'entirely' should provoke the correct knee-jerk reaction – 'not entirely', as the reasons will be more complex than that. Naturally the Liberals who kept Labour in power would not wish to facilitate such Labour commitments as nationalisation. But some would argue that MacDonald was more interested in foreign than domestic affairs, and that while a theoretical socialist he was not committed to specific socialist measures. Colleagues such as Snowden, who might have pushed MacDonald into them, were hidebound by their commitment to orthodox economics, and anyway felt that socialism would have to wait until the budget was balanced and the pound was secure. The economic whirlwind that hit the second government created conditions hostile to socialist experiment, and it should not be forgotten that neither government was long enough in office to embark on an effective socialist programme. Of course, in agreeing to form a minority government, contrary to his previously declared resolution not to, MacDonald was implicitly accepting the Liberal constraints on his legislative programme.

14 Consider the view that in the years between the wars women were still little better than second-class citizens.

Here the theme is women, 1919–39, but the focus is on the extent to which they could be classed as second-class citizens. It might be argued that, theoretically at least, they were now the equals of men in political rights (from 1928), but that there were still barriers to their achieving real equality even here. Yet in other aspects, social, matrimonial, and in jobs, there is a considerable element of the truth in the statement.

15 'MacDonald placed his country before his party, Baldwin placed his party before his country.' Do you agree?

Here a comparison of the two is obviously required. An end-to-end treatment of both men might be weak in elements of comparison; a point-by-point comparison could well be much more effective. Thus taking in turn their personalities, their party leadership and attitude to colleagues, their handlings of international questions, and their attitude to domestic problems – particularly the General Strike and the 1931 crisis – should keep the essay moving along the right lines. Some issues, such as the Abdication Crisis, will not easily fit a point-by-point scheme based on events, but fall naturally into a discussion of methods. Issues such as MacDonald's alleged betrayal of his party and Baldwin's patent honesty or deviousness are implicit here. It would seem unlikely, in any case, that the judgement offered in the question could be accepted without qualification.

16 Was there no alternative to a National Government in 1931?

This, and the following five questions are all of the judgement type. It is important to discuss the circumstances of 1931: the Labour government was not fundamentally divided on the need to protect the pound and balance the budget – it had earlier rejected radical solutions such as those of Mosley and Keynes – so the issue was not whether to make economies, but how much economy to make. Was the gap between what MacDonald and Snowden were urging and what colleagues were prepared to concede unbridgeable? If so, the government could not survive. This always presumes that it was necessary for the government to accede to the bankers' terms, but the alternative seemed to be an unstoppable run on the pound. Until virtually the eve of the Coalition Baldwin and Chamberlain expected to be in power with a minority government, and Labour MPs might have been prepared to allow such a government to make the cuts they would not allow their own government to make. But such a government would have lacked authority, might have been shortlived, and might have been too weak to cope with the crisis. The idea of National Government had been floated several times in 1930 and 1931:

to the majority of the country at large and to the King it seemed the ideal solution, and it lifted an unwelcome task from Baldwin and Chamberlain. Historians can offer, with hindsight, several ways out of the crisis: at the time National Government seemed the best and by far the most feasible option.

17 'As the monarchy had no political power, the Abdication Crisis of 1936 had no contemporary or historic importance.' Do you agree?

The theme here is the combined one of monarchy/abdication, but the focus is on the importance or otherwise of the Abdication Crisis. You might explore the power of the monarchy in the twentieth century, and perhaps challenge the view that it had *no* political power (e.g. the Parliament Crisis 1910–11, the choice of Baldwin in 1923, the formation of the National Government in 1931, and even the alleged part played by Edward VII in cementing the Entente). You should then focus on the crisis of 1936 – its implications for the British Empire, for relations between Church and State, the opportunity it gave to de Valera, its social implications, and you could well conclude that the quotation is over-dismissive of the abdication's importance.

18 'The National Governments of 1931–40 were merely Conservative governments in disguise.' Do you agree?

While the theme is the National Governments, the focus is on the word Conservative. The domination of Conservatives in the support for the governments, especially after the election in October 1931, is obvious. However, some attention should be given to the shrunken band of MacDonald Labour supporters, and to the National Liberals, soon admittedly to be virtually indistinguishable from Conservatives. Consideration of the work of the governments is unlikely to suggest bi- or multi-partisanship: there was nothing specifically socialist, although marketing schemes and state-urged cartels seemed strangely un-Conservative, and London transport and British Airways had a sniff of nationalisation about them. Tariff reform seemed to negate any link with liberalism, and in fact alienated some National Liberal and National Labour support. Most of the domestic work of these governments seemed in keeping with conservatism in that it was cautious and limited. It is also worthwhile to consider whether Chamberlain and Baldwin were not the real power in the land, even before MacDonald's withdrawal from the scene in 1935. The general election of 1935 barely preserved the fiction that a national, rather than Conservative, government was asking for continued support.

19 'An irresponsible and unprincipled politician.' Is this a valid judgement on Churchill's political career, 1918–39?

The theme is Churchill, 1918–39, but the focus is on his alleged irresponsibility and lack of principle. Here points for and against must be considered and a balanced judgement attempted. A double focus is required: Churchill is accused both of lack of principle and irresponsibility: his change of party, the return to the Gold Standard, his attitudes towards India, his exclusion from the National Government, his involvement in the Abdication Crisis, his demand for rearmament and his hostility to appeasement – all need attention. The judgement seems harsh, and it is worth remembering that the two pejorative words clash somewhat: an unprincipled seeker after power does not necessarily behave irresponsibly.

20 'The National Governments neither helped nor hindered the recovery from the Depression.' Do you agree?

The theme is recovery from the Depression and the focus is on whether the National Governments helped or hindered it. Obviously it is essential to analyse the reasons for the recovery in order to assess the governments' part: the abandonment of the Gold Standard, low interest rates (however accidentally tumbled upon as an instrument of policy), the cutting of the budget deficit – all played some part in restoring confidence. The various other reforms have been criticised as too timid and irrelevant to a recovery which mainly came from a house-building boom, and a rise in consumer spending. Efforts to deal with intractable structural unemployment were bound to end in failure. Don't forget to examine whether the government hindered recovery – some historians argue that the National Governments provided merely a favourable climate in which self-recovery could take place. However, few would assert, save in one or two specific instances, that they actually obstructed recovery.

21 Did living standards rise or fall during the 1930s?

This has been the subject of much argument. It is necessary to consider whether cuts in benefit and the means test made the unemployed worse off – possibly marginally so while prices were still falling until 1933, but more rapidly afterwards, except that the means test was in many areas less rigorously applied from 1934 onwards. Of course, anyone becoming unemployed enjoyed lower living standards, but unemployment was falling from 1933. For those in work standards seem to have risen: wages fell but not as fast as prices to 1933, and prices rose but not as fast as wages after it. There is a general consensus that much of the recovery was led by a boom in consumer spending, and consumption was increasing per capita, both of basics and luxuries. Goods were available in wider variety, and domestic equipment and entertainment were well represented in the new industries. The stereotype of the 1930s, with its poverty and hunger marches, certainly needs qualification.

22 To what extent had Britain recovered from the Depression by 1939?

This question has a different focus from Question 20. There the focus was on the governments' contribution to recovery, here it is on the extent of the recovery. This sort of question requires a balanced approach, with consideration of points both ways. You may be able to show a decline in unemployment figures, the recovery of the building trade, the growth of new industries encouraged by the beginnings of protection and low interest rates, and a slow recovery of prices. But you would need to point out the continued weakness in the traditional industries, the fact that unemployment was still high in many areas despite a significant fall nationally, that low wages and lack of public spending restricted demand (limiting but not preventing a rise in consumer spending), and the minimal and permissive nature of much of the government legislation. Full recovery came only with rearmament and war.

23 Were the governments of the Second World War more effective in handling the domestic economy than those of the First?

Note that a comparison is required, and it should not be difficult to tackle topics point by point, e.g. war production and direction of labour, rationing, control of prices and money supply, interest rates and overseas investment, imports and exports, industrial strife, and protection of industry from air attacks. It might well be argued that during the First World War the government acquired a policy by trial and error and that the Second War benefited from what had been learnt. Even so, A.J.P Taylor argues that this often meant the repetition of errors rather than a new approach, and it should be remembered that even in the Second World War much of the government control which regulated the economy was delayed until 1941.

Specimen Essay Answer

(See page 92)

The answer below is not a model answer, nor does it necessarily suggest the only approach. Nevertheless it is an answer which focuses on the question and does represent the type of answer which may be written under examination conditions in about 45 minutes.

Sydney Webb in 1901 called the Liberal Party obsolescent. How far was this a reasonable judgement on the state of the Liberal Party in 1901?

Webb's comment may well have had an ulterior motive. His Fabianism would have found the Liberal Party unreceptive to the radical yet evolutionary reform he was envisaging. If one road to progress was Lib-Labism, alternative routes such as Fabianism, the SDF and the new Labour Representation Committee of 1900 offered better prospects. So Webb's remark seems dismissive of the notion that working men had much to hope for from the Liberal Party, and in a sense was made to justify Fabian support for separate working-class representation in Parliament.

Webb's analysis seemed in 1901 to have more than merely superficial justification. The Liberal Party had been forged by Gladstone from a combination of the 'old' Whigs and 'new' radicals. It had worked well within limits but it had never been an entirely happy partnership, and the Whig element which in the 1860s had had misgivings over the extension of the franchise was still there in the 1890s. Lord Rosebery, and even Sir William Harcourt (despite his death duties), had a patrician attitude to labour questions, and the Conservative Party seemed to have as good a record as the Liberals in promoting local democracy, working-class compensation and insurance, and in advocating old age pensions and female suffrage.

Part of the problem was *laisser-faire*. All the time the Liberals were tied to *laisser-faire* they not only supported free trade in a period when the advantages of this policy were being rapidly eroded by foreign competition, but they were also committed to oppose state intervention, even when state intervention was the only answer to social evils. The increasing impact of the State on the lives of ordinary people led Conservatives to comment 'We are all socialists now', but it was not a description which *laisser-faire* Liberals could relish.

So the Liberals appeared to be hamstrung by Whiggism and *laisser-faire* and seemed to be backward rather than forward looking; they also appeared to be a regional party. In the elections of 1895 and 1900 they would have been virtually wiped out as a political party had it not been for the high Liberal representation in Scotland and Wales. In England, which Lord Rosebery himself had, in an unguarded moment, described as the 'dominant partner' in the union, liberalism appeared to have been judged by the electorate as irrelevant to the problems of the late nineteenth century, and liberalism's last haunt was the Celtic fringe.

One of these problems had been Home Rule for Ireland. The issue had split in the Liberals and so weakened them that from 1886–1905 they, with Irish Nationalist support, could manage only three years in office. Home Rule had provided the Conservative Party with a welcome infusion of Liberal Unionists and had saddled the Liberal Party with the albatross of commitment to an independent Ireland. This was unpopular in England, and helped to destroy the Liberal political base there; it embarrassed many leading Liberals like Lord Rosebery, who had publicly made his support for it conditional upon support for it in England. Other Liberal imperialists similarly squared it with their consciences.

Of course Home Rule and imperialism were irreconcileable. One of Disraeli's legacies had been to infect the Liberal Party with imperialism. Imperialists in the Cabinet had forced Gladstone belatedly to send help to General Gordon in 1884, and while Liberals disliked the Conservative Party for making political capital out of the Boer War, the Liberal-imperialists found the anti-war sentiment of men such as Lloyd George just as distasteful and unacceptable. In the 'khaki' election of 1900 the electorate, buoyed up by 'jingoism', decisively rejected the divided Liberal Party. The party appeared dispirited and demoralised; it certainly lacked a sense of direction. Sydney Webb could hardly be blamed for his comment.

Yet there was in it an element of wishful thinking, possibly tinged with regret. The Liberals appeared to be a dying party. They could therefore be of little use to the working-classes and thus separate representation was a necessity. Webb, in 1901, cannot be blamed for failing to detect within the Liberal Party the seeds of revival and renewal. The mood of the country was changing: when imperialism was at its height, the electorate did not trust the Liberals to carry out imperialist policies, but once imperialism was questioned, as it began to be from the turn of the century, one barrier to supporting the Liberals was removed. Now it was the Conservatives rather than the Liberals who appeared to be backward-looking. The Home Rule issue, which had divided the party, ceased to take centre stage; the dying down of Irish agitation seemed to make it less of an immediate problem. As for radicalism, dynamic men like Lloyd George, rather than the shrinking Whig remnant, seemed likely to give the party its sense of direction, and a revitalised Newcastle programme, geared to the needs of the 1900s rather than the 1890s, was an increasing possibility. *'Laisser-faire'* was buried under radical promises which, when carried out, were to lay the foundations of the welfare state. In 1901 Webb thought of the Liberal Party as deeply divided; within a year Chamberlain was to open a split in the Conservative Party on tariff reform. The Liberal Party could hardly fail to take advantage of it: all could unite behind the rallying cry of free trade and the Liberal divisions were by now little more than personal animosities and rivalries; the Conservative split was on a fundamental issue of policy.

So it seems that Webb was mistaken: he saw the Liberal autumn and winter, but not the Liberal 'Indian summer'. Yet of course it was only an Indian summer. 'Obsolescent' was, in the short term, a mistaken term, but in the long term Webb was prophetic, even if the reasons for his prophecy do not always stand up to close scrutiny.

BIBLIOGRAPHY

There are extensive bibliographies on Britain 1900–1945 in many specialist books. Oddly enough, there is a lack of recent books suitable for A level students, and some of the older works are still valuable.

L. C. B. Seaman: *Post-Victorian Britain 1902–1951* (Methuen, University Paperback 1970). This book is readable and scholarly and gives a good survey of the main themes.

C. L. Mowat: *Britain Between the Wars 1918–40* (Methuen, University Paperback 1968). This is very detailed, and a standard work for all students of the period. Its flowing style and touches of whimsical humour make it readily accessible.

A. J. P Taylor: *English History, 1914–1945* (Pelican 1970). The standard Oxford History, provocative and contentious in places, but worth persevering with even if his obsession with paradox becomes a little irritating on occasions.

Among more recent publications specifically for A level there is:

W. O. Simpson: *Changing Horizons, 1914–80* (Stanley Thornes 1986). This gives a useful survey, explores controversies, and offers and uses extracts from sources both primary and secondary.

Books such as the above should be supplemented by more specialist reading, particularly biography, but monographs on specific issues can be valuable. The following is a brief selection from those which are most useful:

A. Calder: *The People's War: Britain 1939–1945* (Cape 1969) tackles the social and economic aspects of the war.

S. Constantine: *Unemployment between the Wars* (Longman Seminar Series 1980) discusses the problem of unemployment and the varied suggestions for tackling it.

G. Dangerfield: *The Damnable Question* (Constantine 1977) deals with twentieth-century Ireland in the latter part of the book, but tends to be less than charitable to Lloyd George.

D. Marquand: *Ramsay MacDonald* (Cape 1977) Most biographies, like this one, are quite lengthy, but this is interesting in that it offers a vigorous defence of MacDonald against the usual accusations.

H. Pelling: *A Short History of the Labour Party* (Macmillan 1969). A useful and manageable survey.

ACKNOWLEDGEMENTS

The publishers wish to thank the following for their permission to reproduce copyright illustrations:

Labour Party Library, cover.
Punch Publications p.11; p.42; p.47; p.74; p.76; p.77; p.78; p.79; p.80; p.82
David Low, Evening Standard/Centre for the Study of Cartoon and Caricature, University of Kent at Canterbury p.43; p.67.
Express Newspapers p.81 both, p.83 top.

The publishers would like to thank the following for permission to reproduce material in this volume:

Bloomsbury Publishing Ltd for the extract taken from *Waiting for the All Clear*, Ben Wicks (1990); Constable Publishers for the extract from *Memories of Midlands Politics*, F. A. Channing; Eyre & Spottiswoode for the extract from *The Unknown Prime Minister*, R. Blake; John Murray (Publishers) Ltd for the extract from Success in *Twentieth Century World Affairs*, J. B. Watson; Methuen & Co for the extracts from *Post Victorian Britain 1902–51*, L. C. B. Seaman, *Britain Between the Wars 1918–40*, C. L. Mowat (1955) and *Modern England 1885–1945*, J. A. R. Marriott; Oxford University Press for the extract from *English History* 1914–45, A. J. P. Taylor (1965); Simon & Schuster Young Books, Hemel Hempstead for the articles from *Purnell's History of the Twentieth Century* (1969);

Every effort has been made to trace and acknowledge ownership of copyright. The publishers will be glad to make suitable arrangements with any copyright holders whom it has not been possible to contact.

INDEX